I am a Kid for Nature

MY NAME IS

I LIVE AT

MY TOTEM ANIMAL IS

this is my book

Saturday January 1 *New Year's Day* **Sunday January 2**	## Make an Animal Friend Do you have a totem animal? If not, you should. A totem is a special friend. It is a creature that you like a lot. Think about all the animals, bugs, and birds you know and choose one. Learn all you can about your totem. Make a drawing of it. Find out where it lives and what it does for a living.

Twenty feet below the surface of the earth the seasons are reversed. It's coldest there in June and warmest in January because soil is slow to change temperature. The cold of winter doesn't add up until early summer, and the effect of hot weather doesn't show until the air is cold again.

A farm manual of 1815 speaks of a hen-house with "an over-hanging roof that slants upward, which lets the low winter sun in and keeps the high summer sun out." This is still good advice for people who want to use the sun's energy to heat their houses.

Many large animals of the ocean feed on "plankton." This is a term that includes all sorts of sea animals and plants too small or weak to do anything but drift with the current.

The sun's energy must pass through more atmosphere in winter because the tilt of the earth is away from the sun. The sun appears lower in the sky. The atmosphere causes less solar energy to reach the earth and is one reason why winter is cold.

Stars twinkle because the light from them has to pass through the earth's thick atmosphere.

The largest animal that ever lived is living now: it's the blue whale, which grows to 95 feet long and 150 tons.

Emperor penguins dive as deep as 885 feet in their hunt for fish and squid to eat. These birds can stay underwater for as long as 18 minutes.

Monday January 3

Tuesday January 4

Last Quarter Moon
Wednesday January 5

Thursday January 6

Friday January 7

Saturday January 8

Sunday January 9

THE BUG OF THE YEAR

Sow Bug

See that old board lying there on the ground half-covered with grass? Lift it up and peek under. Bet you'll see the Bug of the Year right there in your own backyard! A sow bug, sometimes called pill bug, or wood louse, this bug isn't a bug at all! It is a member of the order Isopoda and is actually related to the crayfish! The sow bug even breathes through gills, like an underwater creature does. That's why it seeks out damp places (such as under that board). In a dry place it would soon die.

Sow bugs are harmless, useful creatures. Some people regard them as pests, and they sometimes do damage young plants by crawling around in the soil among tender roots. But they are garden scavengers. They help feed the soil by breaking up decaying matter. They do not bite people. In fact, they are quite shy and will roll into tiny balls if handled.

The shell of the sow bug is in plates, or segments, which enable it to roll up into a ball. They have seven legs, antennae, or "feelers," and compound eyes. Sow bugs mate in the spring. The female carries her eggs in a pouch under her body. In about six or seven weeks the young hatch and come out of the pouch looking just like adult sow bugs, only smaller. They have an average lifespan of three years.

Make a Sow Bug Farm

Spend a week with the Bug of the Year! You can do just that by making a temporary sow bug farm in a big glass jar. Start with a clean jar that has a wide mouth. Now, put into that jar just what sow bugs like best, and the only way you can do that is to find a place where they already live and look carefully. Is the place wet or just damp? Does the wind blow there? Is it sunny, or shady?

With a trowel carefully dig some of the soil, being sure to get sow bugs along with the dirt. Line the bottom of the jar with a thick layer of dead leaves or grass. Put the soil in next, to a depth of at least three inches. Put more grass and leaves on the top. Put a small rock on the very top. Then put on a lid, but be sure it is punched with small holes.

Put your sow bug farm in a quiet place away from bright light. Don't disturb it for a couple of days. If the soil looks dry, sprinkle a little water on top. After a couple of days, examine the jar carefully.

Dogs have been living with people for about 50,000 years. Cats have been kept around people for at least 5,000 years. While dogs are social animals that really enjoy being with humans, cats keep more of their wild and separate ways.

Uranus spins very rapidly on its side. On some days there the sun would seem to move in a circle in the sky.

The temperature of the air around you helps determine how cold you feel. So does the strength of the wind; stronger winds carry your body heat away faster, making you feel colder. A temperature of 20° F. with a 20-mile-per-hour wind blowing feels about the same as -10° F. with no wind. Weather reports often mention this "windchill factor."

More windchill examples: 35° F. with a 10-mile-per-hour wind feels like 22° F.; 30° F. with a 30-mile-per-hour wind feels like -2° F.

Snow is not an excellent source of water because a great deal of it must be swallowed in order to get a small amount of liquid. The body is chilled by it too.

Hoop Snake

THERE ARE TALES OF A SNAKE THAT PROPELS ITSELF BY PUTTING ITS TAIL IN ITS MOUTH AND ROLLING LIKE A HOOP. CAN YOU TRACE, CUT UP, AND REASSEMBLE THIS SNAKE SO THAT IT CAN ROLL AFTER YOU?

Monday January 10

Tuesday January 11

Kids for Nature Contests deadline is February 20. See page 89.

Wednesday January 12

Thursday January 13

New Moon
●

Friday January 14

Saturday January 15

Martin Luther King, Jr.'s, Birthday

Sunday January 16

Monday January 17	
Tuesday January 18	
Wednesday January 19	
Thursday January 20	
Friday January 21	
Saturday January 22 First Quarter Moon ◑	
Sunday January 23	

You and every other human have 206 bones in your body. The thigh bone is longest; the 3 little bones deep inside your ear are the smallest.

The place where penguins gather to breed is called a "rookery." It needs to be far enough inland from the ocean edge of Antarctica so that ice breaking off does not carry the rookery out to sea. As many as 100,000 birds may gather at breeding time, keeping one another warm by huddling very close together.

Clouds at night trap the earth's heat. On a clear night more heat escapes, so the temperature is lower.

A blanket of snow really is a blanket. It holds in the warmth of the earth and protects against the frost of winter air. Where there is no snow, the soil freezes to a much greater depth. Snow brings down nutrients from the air and spreads them on the ground like fertilizer.

Some flowers put out rotten odors to attract flies to pollinate them. One such species bloomed in a greenhouse in frigid Wyoming in January. The stink was enough to wake the flies out of their hibernation.

The stars are moving. Over a long, long time the constellations change shape.

The layers of snow and ice in glaciers can be read like the rings of a tree or like the layers of soil and rock in a mine. All yield valuable information about conditions on earth in the past.

A bird called the "storm petrel" spends nearly all its life in the air. It will be at sea, hundreds of miles from land, for months, feeding on the tiny ocean organisms called plankton. Storm petrels come ashore only to breed. They have very weak legs and shuffle along the ground using their wings as crutches.

When snow accumulates deep enough, it packs itself into ice and inches forward as a glacier. An iceberg is an enormous chunk of glacier that breaks off and floats freely in the ocean.

Snow is so much a part of their lives that Eskimos have many words for it. They call snow not yet picked up by wind api. Snow that has been worked by the wind and piled into a firm mass is upsik. When it moves along the ground, it is siqoq.

Not only people, but animals, too, like to play in snow. A polar bear will catch its cub at the bottom of a snow slide. A troop of monkeys called "macaques" were brought from Japan to Oregon, where they saw and touched snow for the first time. They made snowballs by rolling snow, but then instead of throwing them, they sat on them.

All animals need salt in some form. Salt helps control the flow of water through the body's tissues and aids in digestion.

Certain whales have baleen instead of teeth. Baleen hangs down from the upper jaw like a huge brush. The whales use it like a strainer to gather small fish and plankton from the water.

After the female penguin has laid her single egg, the male takes over for the nine weeks until it hatches. The male holds the egg and keeps it warm with a special flap of skin on his lower abdomen. He does not eat during this period and is blasted by the Antarctic weather. The female, meanwhile, has gone on a long trip to the ocean for food. The male may lose half his body weight before she returns.

Monday January 24

Tuesday January 25

Wednesday January 26

Thursday January 27

Full Moon
○ **Friday January 28**

Saturday January 29

Sunday January 30

How Many Birds Can You Find Hidden in This Picture?

February 2 On Groundhog Day, the legend says, the groundhog wakes from its long winter sleep and crawls to the entrance of its burrow. If it can see its shadow — if it's sunny, that is — the prediction is for bad weather yet to come, and the groundhog goes back to sleep for another six weeks. Groundhogs are also called "woodchucks."

Snow that lies a long time at high elevations in the Rocky Mountains is colored watermelon-red by an alga. Another kind of alga in the area of Yellowstone National Park colors snow green.

Some fish are covered with round scales that have rings on them. By counting these rings, just as with a tree, you can discover how old the fish is.

What did the ocean say to the shore? (**Nothing, it just waved.**)

The harvestman has several other common names. Many people call it "daddy longlegs." It is also known as the "quiver" or "shimmy" spider because of the way it shakes up and down in its web. The harvestman, though it has eight legs, is not a true spider. Its body isn't pinched in the middle and divided into two segments like a spider's is.

Hornets and yellow jackets have sharp, smooth stingers, which don't stick in their victims. So these insects can — and do — sting many times without harm to themselves.

There are as many chickens in the world as there are people.

If your legs were as long in relation to your body as the harvestman's legs are to its body, you would be about 40 feet tall.

Monday January 31

Tuesday February 1

Wednesday February 2

Thursday February 3

Last Quarter Moon
Friday February 4

Saturday February 5

Sunday February 6

Monday February 7	An unusual plant common in our central and southern states is the compass plant. It takes its name from the fact that its leaves line up in a north-south direction. Another nickname for it is "polar plant."
Tuesday February 8	**In the dry Gobi Desert of Asia, gazelles rely on buried snow to save them from dying of thirst. Drifts of snow are blown into hollow places and covered by sand a foot or two deep. The sand insulates the snow, keeping it from melting. The gazelles know where to dig for a drink.**
Wednesday February 9	*People are made of the same kinds of atoms that stars are made of. The atoms are just arranged differently.* Arboreal snakes are ones that live in trees. Among these, the best climbers can crawl up a tree holding their bodies nearly straight. They wedge themselves between cracks in the rough bark and inch their way up.
Thursday February 10	Galaxies are groups of stars that look close together in space. (Actually there are tremendous distances between the stars, even though there are "clusters" of them.) Earthlings live in a galaxy called the "Milky Way," which looks like drops of milk spilling across the sky.
Friday February 11	

Saturday February 12   New Moon ●
Lincoln's Birthday

Sunday February 13

Chicken Fences

By drawing only three straight lines you can have each of these chickens in a pen of its own. Can you figure out where to draw the lines?

Because the moon has almost no atmosphere, the temperature on its surface swings much more wildly than on earth. The moon's surface temperature reaches the boiling point of water (212° F.) and drops to -238° F.

The smallest dog is the Chihuahua. Adults weigh only two or three pounds, while puppies can fit in a teacup.

The hog-nosed snake can spread out the ribs high up on its neck and present a frightening hood, like a cobra's. Then it forces its breath out in loud, violent hisses. It may look ferocious, but actually it's defenseless — a a very heavy, stocky, slow snake.

Clouds are masses of water vapor that we can see in the air. Very cold and dry air freezes water vapor into high, thin clouds of ice.

Hospital records seem to show that bleeding increases during the full moon. Police records show that crimes are more numerous during the days right around the full moon. People have long believed that the moon affects moods and actions. The word "lunatic," which means a crazy person, comes from *luna,* the Latin word for moon.

The puffer fish can puff itself up by swallowing either air or water. As a big ball, it's more frightening to its enemies and harder to bite.

The black widow spider really is a widow. She devours the male during their mating.

A very bright star at a greater distance will seem as bright as a weaker but closer star.

Monday February 14
Valentine's Day

Tuesday February 15

Wednesday February 16
Ash Wednesday

Thursday February 17

Friday February 18

Saturday February 19

First Quarter Moon
◑

Sunday February 20

Today is the deadline for contest entries. See page 89.

Raccoon

If you live near the woods or a large park, you may already know the animal of the year. If you live in a big city, you'll find it at the zoo. The raccoon is one of the animals who have learned to live with people as neighbors. Maybe one of the reasons raccoons interest us so is that they act a little like people. They are very agile with their forepaws. In fact, one Indian tribe called the raccoon "he who scratches with his hands." Raccoons are fond of water and often wash their food before eating it. That's why the German word for raccoon means "wash bear."

Raccoons are mischievous and curious. They raid chicken pens and steal eggs (and sometimes chickens). They raid garbage cans for leftovers. They look cute and can be tamed, but behind their twinkling eyes is a nasty temper. Raccoons make a soft churring sound when they are in a good mood, but they squeal and shout like pigs when they fight—which is often.

Raccoons live in hollow trees. They mate in winter, and nine weeks later four or five tiny coons are born. During the coldest winter months, raccoons fall into a deep sleep and live on the fat stored in their tails. They are night creatures, so you will not see them much during daylight hours.

A Late Supper

If you think raccoons may be in your neighborhood, try leaving food outside on the doorstep at night. Pick a place where you can watch from indoors (and maybe turn on an outside light). Raccoons love fruit, especially melon. They also enjoy raw eggs, but be sure not to break the shell. They do that. Don't give up the first night. If they don't come, try again with fresh fruit the next night. If the supper is gone in the morning, it probably means they came while you dozed off.

Putting out hay over snow-covered ground will not help deer. They are not grazing animals like cows, horses, and sheep. They are browsers.

The opossum is famous for its habit of pretending to be dead. This imitation is so convincing that a predator will lose its interest and appetite. Some scientists think the threatened animal is so scared that it actually passes into a coma at those times. Faking death has come to be called "playing 'possum."

ZZZ...HUH?

We may think of bears as sleeping soundly through the winter, but their body temperatures and heart rates don't drop as low as those of true hibernators. Bears can be awakened easily, and they become their normal active selves in a few minutes.

Saturn is the most distant planet you can see without the help of a telescope. It takes Saturn thirty of our Earth years to travel one time around the sun.

An insect doesn't use much food in winter, and the amount of its blood flow can be lowered then. Its heart may even stop pulsing for hours or days, yet the insect will be alive and healthy, just waiting for warm weather, when it will become active again.

You can brush your teeth with salt. It will kill bacteria that live in your mouth.

The chameleon is best known for its ability to change colors. But it can also move each eye in a different direction, letting the chameleon look forward and backward at the same time.

Monday February 21

Washington's Birthday

Tuesday February 22

Wednesday February 23

Thursday February 24

Friday February 25

Saturday February 26

Full Moon ○   **Sunday February 27**

Monday February 28	
Tuesday March 1	
Wednesday March 2	
Thursday March 3	
Friday March 4	
Saturday March 5	
Sunday March 6 Last Quarter Moon ◐	

The sun appears to follow a yearly path among the stars. The zone of the sky in which the path lies is called the "zodiac." The paths of the moon and the other planets lie in this narrow zodiac too. This is one way we know that the solar system is a flat disk shape, like a pancake.

If its threats don't succeed, the hognosed snake will twist and roll over and over until at last, on its back with its mouth open, it makes a "final" twitch. This is another act; it's really "playing 'possum."

These vegetables like to grow in cool weather: peas, radishes, turnips, spinach, lettuce, cauliflower. Some of them don't even mind a frost. Start a garden with them in early spring.

People divide the zodiac into twelve sections with 30 divisions in each one. That's 360 altogether, a complete circle. Each section has the name of the constellation (group of stars) that was closest to that section when the names were given 2,000 years ago. We think of the first section as being the one where the sun appears at the vernal (spring) equinox. It's called "Aries."

We name a wind for the direction *from* which it blows. A north wind is one that blows *from* the north.

Some people believe the sign of the zodiac in which the sun, moon, and planets appeared on the day you were born influenced what kind of personality you have. This belief is called "astrology." Astrologers also advise people about the future by studying the positions of the heavenly bodies. Their predictions are called "horoscopes."

The dolphin is a mammal, which means that it breathes air. But it can hold its breath for six minutes and dive down 100 feet to do its fishing. The ocean water is very cold at that depth; a thick layer of fat beneath the dolphin's skin keeps it warm.

An insect can reverse its heartbeat and cause blood to flow in the opposite direction.

Tri in Latin means three. The many wildflowers named "trillium" all have three sepals, three petals, whorls of three leaves, three-cell ovaries, and three ribs on each berry. Can you find a bouquet of three?

The commonest trillium is the red trillium. Its nicknames tell us lots about it. "Stinking Benjamin" refers to its not-so-sweet scent. "Wake robin" reminds us that it blooms early in spring. Indians and early settlers used it to ease childbirth and called it "birthroot."

When they are out of sight of each other, elephants make a rumbling sound, almost like the purring of a very large cat. If one of them senses danger, it suddenly stops its rumbling noise and warns the rest of the herd by its silence.

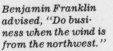

Benjamin Franklin advised, "Do business when the wind is from the northwest."

Peas need cool weather. Plant them early in the spring or late in the summer. With some kinds you eat the pod, with others you eat just the peas inside the pod. The peas are the plant's seeds.

Monday March 7

Tuesday March 8

Wednesday March 9

Thursday March 10

Friday March 11

Saturday March 12

Sunday March 13

Native American Toys

Games and Toys from Sticks and Stones

Double ball stick

Double balls

Native American children loved whirling, spinning toys and games. And they liked to make them as much as they liked to play with them. You can make the same kind of toys. Use toy parts that are all around you. You can change sticks, string, and stones into toys and games without using fancy tools. America's first game players used their play to learn skills that were necessary for hunting and fishing.

Double Ball is a Native American game of catch. The object is to toss a con-nected "double" ball back and forth without touching it with your hands. Use a curved stick to throw and catch the balls. The balls can be beanbags, beads, or even old tennis balls tied together.

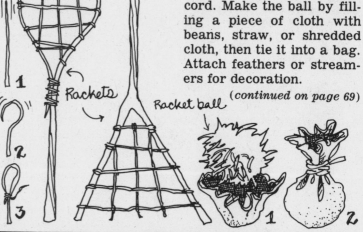

Rackets

Racket ball

Racket Ball is another game of catch. This one uses a netted racket and a soft ball. Make rackets from forked sticks, or you can soak a thin, pliable stick in water overnight, then bend it to make a round racket. Finish the racket by tying a loose net over it with heavy cord. Make the ball by filling a piece of cloth with beans, straw, or shredded cloth, then tie it into a bag. Attach feathers or streamers for decoration.

(continued on page 69)

The fairy tern, a bird that lives near the coast of the Indian Ocean, is the only bird that dares to hatch its egg (it lays only one) high up on a branch *without* a nest.

Even little changes in the earth's climate could cause very big changes for us. If the earth's temperature rose just 2° F., the melting of glaciers and icebergs would raise the level of the oceans and cause flooding in many places around the globe.

The cowbird eats insects that fly up in front of cows' feet. The cowbird female lays her egg in another bird's nest and counts on the other mother to raise her baby.

The ancient Greeks believed the god Aeolus was in charge of all winds. He kept them locked in a cave that had eight openings, each blocked by a big rock. He would roll the rock aside to let out the wind: a slight opening to release a breeze, halfway for a moderate blow, wide open for a storm.

Which side of an ostrich has the most feathers? (The outside.)

Twig Leaper

This twig is a natural hopper. All you need is a stout Y-shaped twig, another short piece of twig, and a fat rubber band.

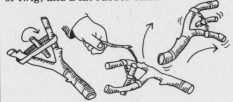

Wind up your leaper and put it on the ground. Gently. You might also need a leaper-nudger, made from a long stick. Sometimes a gentle poke is needed to release the short twig. Make one for a friend and see whose leaper jumps higher, or farther.

New Moon ●

Monday March 14

Tuesday March 15

Wednesday March 16

Thursday March 17

Friday March 18

Saturday March 19

Spring Equinox

Sunday March 20

Monday March 21	First Quarter Moon

Spiders aren't insects. They don't have wings or antennae. They have four, not three, pairs of legs. Not all spiders spin webs.

Tuesday March 22

The eyes of polar bears have a special membrane, the "nictitating" membrane, that passes sideways across the eyeball and clears away slush. Prairie cattle and Arctic sled dogs, whose eyes don't have such equipment, have a much harder time seeing during snowstorms.

Wednesday March 23

At breeding time hornbills find a tree with a hollow, and the female climbs in. Together, she and the male close up the opening with mud, leaving only a tiny hole. The female stays in this dark nest for up to four months while she lays one or two eggs and sits until they hatch.

Thursday March 24

Asteroids are rocks floating in space. They are not ball shaped like the planets; most of them look like cigars. Most of the asteroids whirl around the sun in an orbit between Mars and Jupiter, but some have much different orbits that carry them through more of the solar system and closer to Earth.

Friday March 25

The fastest swimmer in the ocean is the sailfish. Its top speed is about 68 miles per hour. The large fin on its back — its "sail" — is folded flat while the fish swims. The sail is raised for balance when the sailfish slows down.

Saturday March 26

There are breezes, gusts, gales, and winds of every description. Following are the highest wind speeds ever recorded in some windy American locations: Albuquerque, New Mexico, 90 miles per hour; Key West, Florida, 122; Omaha, Nebraska, 109; Cape Hatteras, North Carolina, 110; New Orleans, Louisiana, 98; Galveston, Texas, 100; Mount Washington, New Hampshire, 231!

Sunday March 27
Palm Sunday

In the United States you could enjoy the wonderful feeling of early spring for three whole months, if you moved every day. If you started in the South about March 1 and traveled north about 25 miles each day, you'd catch lilacs and tulips blooming in northern Maine and Minnesota at the end of May.

When the weather reporter says, "One inch of rain fell today," what does that mean? It means enough rain fell to cover one acre of ground one inch deep with water. That's 27,143 gallons.

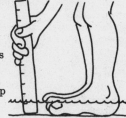

Water always wants to run down: from sky to earth, from mountain to ocean, from soil surface to underground.

Winter snows in the mountains determine the water supply for irrigation and power use. This snow melts in the spring and fills lakes and rivers. If spring comes late, the melting happens faster and can cause floods.

A mother pig, called a "sow," can have as many as 27 piglets in one litter.

Easter is a very important Christian holiday, but the symbols of Easter are much older than Christianity. Long before the time of Jesus, people celebrated the renewal of life at this time of year. The egg is a very old symbol of birth and creation. The hare was an ancient Egyptian symbol of fertility and spring. The Easter egg and the Easter bunny have ancestors!

How do calendar makers decide when Easter is? Easter is the first Sunday following the first full moon after the vernal (spring) equinox.

Full Moon
◯

Monday March 28

Tuesday March 29

First Night of Passover

Wednesday March 30

Thursday March 31

Friday April 1

Good Friday

April Fool's Day

What is Lirpa Loof?
Don't look at page 58.

Saturday April 2

Sunday April 3

Easter Sunday

Monday April 4	
Tuesday April 5	Last Quarter Moon ◑
Wednesday April 6	
Thursday April 7	
Friday April 8	
Saturday April 9	
Sunday April 10	

Flamingo chicks bark like puppies do when they are hungry.

Fruit trees and grapevines are often planted on hillsides because cold air flows downhill. In these places frost is more likely to form in the valleys below than where the trees and vines stand.

Words for animal babies are plentiful in our language. You know that a baby cat is a kitten, but did you know that a baby swan is a cygnet? Here are more: a baby kangaroo is a joey, a baby turkey is a poult, a baby mackerel is a spike or blinker or tinker. Call a baby pig a piglet or a shoat or a farrow. Whelp is the name for a baby dog or tiger; call a baby fox, beaver, rabbit, and cat a kit.

The winds that blow around the equator of Saturn are three times as strong as the ones on Jupiter and ten times fiercer than the hurricane winds on Earth.

What do they call baby cats in Alabama? (Kittens.)

The word "amphibian" means double life, and that's exactly the kind of life this animal has. Part of its life is spent in water, where it can take oxygen from the water through its gills, the way a fish does. Later the amphibian lives on land and uses the lungs it has grown to breathe air. Frogs and toads are amphibians.

Where is the wettest place in the United States? Mt. Waiale-ale (say why-ALAY-alay) on the Hawaiian island of Kauai gets the prize. The average rainfall on that jungly place is 460 inches each year. That's more than 38 feet!

Humidity is water in the air in the form of small droplets that form invisible water vapor. Hot air holds more water vapor than cold air. When hot air meets cold air, water vapor is sometimes squeezed out of it to make rain.

The world's biggest bird eggs are those of the ostrich: up to six inches long, weighing about three pounds, strong enough to support the weight of a full-grown human.

It's estimated that there are three million worms beneath a typical acre of grassland. In just one year these helpful creatures might bring ten tons of soil up to the surface.

An amazing fish is the grunion. The female of this species flops ashore on the beaches of southern California, where, even though she can't breathe out of water, she digs into the sand with her tail and lays about 3,000 eggs. She will do this only at certain times of very high tide, so that later waves will not reach high enough on shore to uncover the eggs. The eggs develop until the next very high tide, when they are swept by the waves out to sea and hatch as baby grunions.

**When apple blossoms bloom at night
For fifteen days, no rain in sight.**

Carrots belong to the same plant family as parsley, celery, and dill (the herb used to make dill pickles). At one time people were interested in this plant only for its value as medicine, not as food.

The ostrich is a giant bird, about nine feet tall and weighing up to 300 pounds. Its wings are too small to lift a bird that large off the ground. The ostrich is a fast runner.

Monday April 11

Tuesday April 12

New Moon
● Wednesday April 13

Thursday April 14

Friday April 15

Saturday April 16

Sunday April 17

Bubbles in the Breeze and Bean Tepees

What could be nicer than lying on your back in the grass and blowing long strings of shiny bubbles into the breeze? Most variety stores sell bubble kits, but you can make better ones yourself. You need bubble juice and a wand.

You can make bubbles simply by using dishwashing soap (detergent), but you'll have better luck if you get a bottle of glycerin from the druggist and add that and some water as well. Pour the glycerin into a fruit jar, then fill the glycerin bottle with detergent and add that. Then add half a bottleful of water. Stir to mix the ingredients. Now, for the wand.

If you want to make giant bubbles, cut the rim from a large plastic container (such as a gallon jar). Add a clothespin for a handle. Also, you can bend wire or make a nifty bubble frame from plastic straws and string. See instructions above.

How about a bubble contest? Who can blow the biggest? Whose bubble will last the longest? Whose will travel farthest? Can you think of other categories?

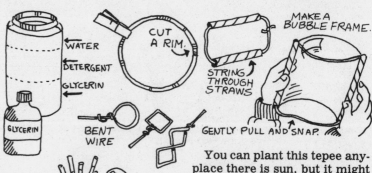

WATER
DETERGENT
GLYCERIN

GLYCERIN

CUT A RIM.

MAKE A BUBBLE FRAME.

STRING THROUGH STRAWS

GENTLY PULL AND SNAP.

BENT WIRE

You can plant this tepee anyplace there is sun, but it might be most fun to plant it smack in the middle of a vegetable garden. *You'll need:* Kentucky Wonder or Sugar Snap or other climbing beans and at least eight bamboo or other poles that are eight feet long. Draw a six-foot circle on the ground and work the soil well just outside the circle. Use a garden fork to loosen the soil to a depth of at least six or eight inches. Get a grownup to help you if the soil is too hard. Next, set up the poles. Arrange them evenly, but leave a larger gap in one place. That will be the door. Push the poles into the loose soil and tie them together at the top.

Now, plant the beans about an inch under the soil at the base of each pole, on the outside. Plant two beans for each pole. Water the ring of loose soil well, then cover it with dry leaves or hay, which will help the soil stay damp. Check every day or two to make sure the soil stays damp. As the young plants develop, make sure each one is touching one of the poles so it will grow up the pole, not across the ground. Soon you'll have a green, leafy, shady hideaway.

LEAVE A GAP IN THE CIRCLE OF BEAN PLANTS FOR YOUR DOOR.

Birds lose and replace their feathers at least once a year. This process is called "molting." Molting usually occurs just after the breeding season, but it doesn't happen all at once. It happens gradually — if a bird lost all its feathers at once, it couldn't fly.

The manatee is a sea mammal that lives in Florida waters. Known as the "sea cow," it grazes on underwater plants (eating as much as 100 pounds a day) and is as gentle as a land cow. The manatee mother's nipple is in her "armpit" — beneath her flipper — so that's where her baby nurses.

The distance through the center of the moon (its diameter) is 2,160 miles. For comparison, consider that the distance from New York to California is about 3,000 miles.

In the famous story, Bambi is often shown living in a dark forest of tall trees. A deer probably would starve in such a location. Deer eat young shoots of trees and bushes, and few young plants can survive where the sun rarely reaches the ground.

Sleeping-Alligator Sneak

Here is an illustration of sleeping alligators. Can you chart a path of two straight lines through the alligators without bumping into (and awakening!) them. You may change your direction only once as you go from the bottom to the top.

	Monday April 18
	Tuesday April 19
First Quarter Moon ◑	Wednesday April 20
	Thursday April 21 *John Muir's Birthday*
	Friday April 22
	Saturday April 23
	Sunday April 24

Monday April 25	
Tuesday April 26	
Wednesday April 27 Full Moon	
Thursday April 28	
Friday April 29	
Saturday April 30	
Sunday May 1 *May Day*	

No vegetable grows as fast as the radish. Some varieties are ready to eat three weeks after planting. Gardeners like this because they can plant radishes to fill in empty areas around the garden.

The name "strawberry" comes from the very old word "strew," which means to spread out. The strawberry plant produces new plants by spreading out runners, which take root nearby. When cut grains are spread out—strewn—and dried, they become hay and *straw*.

Earthworms force their way through soft earth. They must eat their way through harder soil. The earth a worm eats passes through its alimentary canal (digestive system) and is deposited on the ground's surface as castings. Castings improve the ability of soil to grow plants.

Plants turn light energy from the sun into growth energy. If they couldn't perform this miracle, all animals on earth, including us humans, would soon be extinct! The miracle is called "photosynthesis."

Fawns (baby deer) are born with no scent, so their enemies have trouble finding them.

Once on land, most toads stay there the rest of their lives. They hop back to the water only to start a new family.

Blue jays have a reputation as cannibals because they'll eat the eggs and babies of other birds. Most of a blue jay's diet, though, consists of seeds, nuts, acorns, and wild fruit. These noisy birds enjoy making their familiar fuss, but they are also excellent mimics: they can imitate perfectly the calls of many other singing birds.

Some ocean waves are caused by underwater landslides, earthquakes, or even volcanoes. Tides, the effect of the sun and moon, create other waves. But most waves are caused by winds. Sometimes waves will travel thousands of miles from where they got their first windy push.

The mother swan uses down from her body, as well as plants, when she makes her nest.

Some snakes lay eggs, from which babies don't hatch for days. Others, including rattlesnakes, deliver thin-skinned sacs from which the baby snakes hatch almost immediately.

Ducklings swim when they're one day old. A foal (baby horse) can run a few hours after it is born.

The sense of smell brings butterfly and moth mates together. In an experiment some female moths were put in a cage while the males, marked with numbers on their wings, were taken far from the cage and released. Males that were released as far as nine miles downwind could still smell the odor of the females and found their way back with little trouble.

The English writer Izaak Walton said of strawberries, "Doubtless God could have made a better berry, but doubtless God never did."

BUT.... WHO AM I?

WORM ANALYST

A worm is not a snake because it doesn't have a backbone. A worm is not a lizard because it doesn't have legs. Worms do have feet, though. There are little bristles on the underside of each segment of the worm's body. It uses them in crawling.

Monday May 2

Tuesday May 3

Last Quarter Moon
Wednesday May 4

Thursday May 5

Friday May 6

Saturday May 7

Sunday May 8

Making Fly-in Restaurants

and Other Creature-Feeders

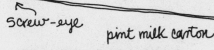

Meet the colorful, friendly birds and bugs who live in your neighborhood. Make a feeder and share a meal with your flying friends.

Keep bird feeders out of the reach of hungry cats and other predators by hanging them from a string. Lightweight feeders made from milk cartons or plastic bottles are cozy eating places and protection from wind and rain.

Make a mobile trolley feeder that you can load at your windowsill, then send it off to a place where birds can eat in privacy. Use a pint milk carton and hang it on a string with large paper clips, as shown.

Make a high-rise bird feeder by using pie plates and a pole, as shown below. A wooden salad bowl also makes a good pole-top feeder, but the simplest feeder of all is a plumber's helper set in the ground.

(continued on page 64)

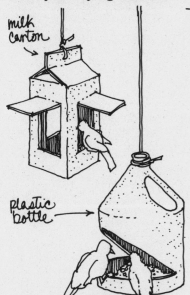

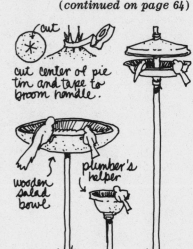

cut center of pie tin and tape to broom handle.

Certain kinds of plants seem to enjoy growing next to certain other kinds. Both grow better together than they do apart. Gardeners take advantage of this fact; "companion planting" is putting these good friends together in the garden. Corn and beans are good companions. Other plants aren't so friendly to each other. The wrong combinations seem to cause these plants to be weak. Many gardeners don't plant peas near onions for this reason.

The adult mayfly has no mouth, only traces of mouthparts, which don't work. These adults live only a few hours; most of a mayfly's life is spent in its nymph, or immature, form.

What is gray and has four legs and a trunk? (A mouse going on vacation.)

Baby snakes have an "egg tooth," a tiny, sharp projecting tip to the snout. Baby birds have something similar, and both lose them quickly after hatching. With its egg tooth, a baby snake cuts its way out of the egg. A bird chick uses its built-in tool to knock and break its egg from inside.

The African elephant is the largest land animal in the world. Just the ears alone of the bull (male) measure four feet across. He's about ten feet tall at the shoulders and weighs about six tons.

These vegetables like to grow in hot weather: tomatoes, peppers, corn, squash, melons, beans. They need fairly warm nights and hot days. Don't plant them too early.

Metamorphosis is the word that describes the big changes many animals go through between their babyhood and adulthood. Caterpillars become butterflies, and tadpoles become frogs or toads. These are examples of metamorphosis.

Monday May 9

Tuesday May 10

Wednesday May 11

New Moon
● Thursday May 12

Friday May 13

Saturday May 14

Sunday May 15

27

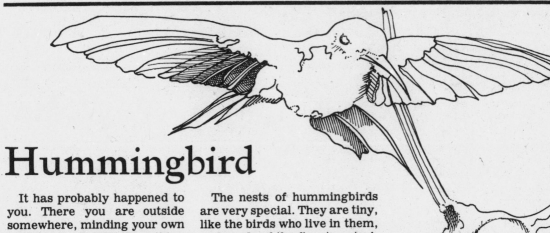

Hummingbird

It has probably happened to you. There you are outside somewhere, minding your own business, and ZIP! Something flashes by so fast all you see is a blur. It makes a sound like a tiny helicopter. It must be a hummingbird!

The smallest hummingbird is not much larger than a bumblebee. The fastest hummingbirds are too fast to even see. Their wings move at 60 miles per hour. Hummingbird tongues are so long they have to curl them up inside the backs of their heads. Those tongues, like hoses, are hollow for sucking up sweet nectar from deep inside the throats of flowers. Hummingbirds can hover in midair because their shoulder joints rotate. Turned one way, the wings propel the bird forward. Turned the other, they allow it to hover or fly straight up. Just like a helicopter. Amazing, isn't it? Hummingbirds are tiny, but they are tough. Some of them migrate every year for long distances over ocean waters. And they are beautiful. Have you ever seen such colors on any other bird?

The nests of hummingbirds are very special. They are tiny, like the birds who live in them, and made of the finest materials. Cocoon threads, spider silk, cattail down. Only the softest, finest things will do. Hummingbirds hide their nests well and often return year after year to the same place to raise a family. If you find such a nest, peek but don't disturb. If it is occupied, watch only from a distance.

Lunch on the Wing

Special hummingbird feeders are inexpensive and widely available. Try pet shops or garden supply stores. If you keep one filled near a window, you will be rewarded during spring and summer months by regular hummingbird visits.

The star closest to Earth (it's called Alpha Centauri) is about 7,000 times as far away from us as the most distant planet (Pluto).

Birds can't stand the taste of monarch butterflies, which taste the way they do because they ate milkweed when they were larvae (baby stage). Since the viceroy butterfly looks very much like the monarch, birds avoid it also, even though it is, to birds, quite tasty.

The larvae of one species of wasp must eat insect meat as soon as they hatch from eggs. When the mother wasp can't find a supply of insects, the eggs hatch inside her body, and the larvae soon eat her alive!

What goes ZZUB, ZZUB, ZZUB? (A bee flying backwards.)

Tornadoes occur most often east of the Rocky Mountains, especially in the drainage basin of the Mississippi River. They have been recorded in every month, but are most frequent in late spring and early summer.

Tornadoes are always associated with thunderstorms. Some of them turn clockwise, but all *hurricanes* turn counterclockwise. *Tornadoes* come in families; *hurricanes* usually develop as single storms. A *tornado* usually lasts only a few minutes and travels less than ten miles. A *hurricane* lasts for days and travels thousands of miles.

The total energy of a major thunderstorm is greater than that of an atomic bomb. The electrical energy of lightning is enormous, but it lasts such a very short time that we can't use it for our electrical needs on earth.

	Monday May 16
	Tuesday May 17
	Wednesday May 18
First Quarter Moon ◑	**Thursday May 19**
	Friday May 20
	Saturday May 21
	Sunday May 22

Monday May 23	
Tuesday May 24	
Wednesday May 25	
Thursday May 26	Full Moon
Friday May 27	
Saturday May 28	
Sunday May 29	

Ants, bees, and wasps can make taste tests with their antennae. In some butterflies and the honeybee, the tarsal, or foot, joints have a set of taste buds. These insects know if materials are edible without putting them in their mouths.

Lupine is a member of the pea family, which includes clovers and beans too. An old nickname for lupine is "wolf's bean."

A black panther is really an all-black leopard. Black panthers often have babies that look like most leopards, with bright yellow, spotted coats.

Some of the enormous damage a tornado causes comes from windows popping out, barns exploding, and roofs blowing off. These things happen because air pressure in tornadoes, as in the center of hurricanes, is very low. When the tornado hits, suddenly the pressure outside a building will be much less than the normal pressure inside, a difference great enough to push out windows.

The European cuckoo lays her egg in the nest of some other bird. Like the cowbird, she flies away while another sits on her egg.

Who Is Frannie Feeding?

An adult worm has about 115 segments, or divisions, along its body. Its brain is located in segment three. Its heart lies between segments five and eleven. Its mouth is between segment one and the worm's knob end.

Farmers and gardeners are helped by knowing facts about what kind of weather they can expect. Records kept over many years help predict when the last plant-killing frost is likely to occur in the spring, how much rain will fall each month, how hot it will get in the summer, and much more.

Even while it is being carried away in the jaws of an enemy, a minnow will release a scent that alerts others nearby. When a bee stings an enemy, it gives off an odor that calls other bees to the attack.

The name "daisy" is a contraction of "day's eye." The little pink and white English daisy closes up at sunset and opens again at sunrise: an eye of the day.

When ditch and pond offend the nose Look for rain and stormy blows.

It was once a custom never to throw a plum or peach pit away, but to properly bury it, with hopes that a fruit tree would spring up and survive there.

Marsupials are an unusual family of animals whose females have a pouch in which their young go on developing after birth. Kangaroos are marsupials; so are opossums, the only example to be found in North America. When the opossum baby has grown too big to stay in its mother's pouch, it rides with her by clinging to her back and tail.

Monday May 30
Memorial Day

Tuesday May 31

Wednesday June 1

Thursday June 2

Last Quarter Moon
Friday June 3

Saturday June 4

Sunday June 5

Monday June 6	
Tuesday June 7	
Wednesday June 8	
Thursday June 9	
Friday June 10 New Moon ●	
Saturday June 11	
Sunday June 12	

Mosquitoes are attracted to their victims by body temperature. Many birds have body temperatures higher than a human's. So some kinds of mosquitoes that are attracted to these birds would never bite you because you're too cool.

When the archer fish sees an insect or a spider above the water, it spits out drops of water and knocks down its prey. It can spit as far as 25 inches.

A shrew cannot go without eating for more than a few hours. Its little body burns up fuel so fast that it must be supplied with food almost constantly. To meet this need, the shrew has developed remarkable courage and ferocity. It will attack and quickly kill creatures many times its own size.

Most of the casualties of the Spanish-American War (1898) were caused not by bullets but by the yellow-fever mosquito.

When the toad swallows, its eyes sink into its head and help push the food down its throat.

Sometimes plants will tell by the way they grow what minerals are in the earth beneath them. The roots of herbs, shrubs, and trees absorb minerals and use them to manufacture leaves, stems, flowers, and seeds. Different minerals—including silver and gold—produce different shapes, colors, and other qualities in plant parts. If you know how to look, you can go prospecting with plants.

Lightning causes thunder. It is electricity, which, as in a light bulb, creates heat as well as light. Air heated by lightning is suddenly packed together and creates waves of sound that we call thunder.

The Great Summer City
Treasure Hunt
and other hot weather entertainments
or -- this year, no vacation blahs

You could do this any time of year, but it sounds like more fun when the days are long, the streets are warm and dry, and you've got some time on your hands. So round up some friends, get out on the sidewalk, and see how much nature you can find in the city.

It's best to divide up into teams of two each. That's more fun, and besides, two heads are better than one. Here is a sample list, but you could invent your own. Give yourselves a time limit, say, one afternoon. The team back soonest with the most items wins. Wins what? Well, you decide that too, but do it ahead of time so everyone knows the prize at the start.

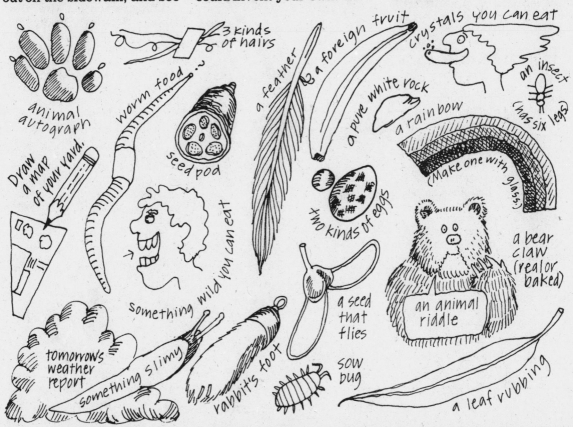

animal autograph

Draw a map of your yard.

worm food

3 kinds of hairs

seed pod

a feather

a foreign fruit

a pure white rock

a rainbow

crystals you can eat

an insect (has six legs)

two kinds of eggs

(Make one with glass)

something wild you can eat

a bear claw (real or baked)

an animal riddle

tomorrow's weather report

something slimy

rabbit's foot

a seed that flies

sow bug

a leaf rubbing

The Icky Stickies

How much heat can you take? As it turns out, you can take quite a lot. Humans can survive several hours at up to 200° F. with no serious effects, *provided it's heat in a dry environment*. When air is damp and humid, it's another story. The high humidity throws a wrench into your body's cooling system.

Air can only absorb a limited amount of water. On days when the humidity is high, the air has as much water as it can hold. Sweat stacks up on your skin because the air can't absorb it fast enough. Since the evaporation of sweat is what keeps you cool, you feel hot and sticky. Ugh!

Breeze Machine

When you perspire on a hot day, the air around you absorbs your moisture and becomes humid. If there is no breeze to move the air, you can make your own. A fan will help you trade the sweaty, close air for air that's farther away—and drier. *You'll need:* a sheet of letter-size paper, a strip of cardboard, and a stapler.

Fold the paper accordion-style, then fold it in half. Fold the cardboard strip in half too, and put the ends over the squeezed end of the fan. Staple on the handle through the fan.

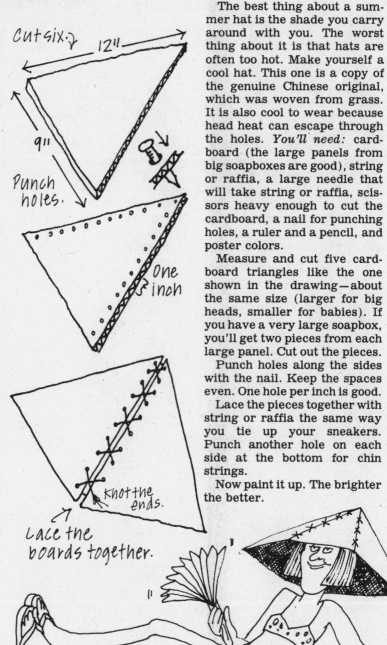

Cut six.
12"
9"
Punch holes.
One inch
Knot the ends.
Lace the boards together.

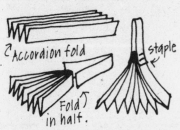

Accordion fold
Fold in half.
staple

Soapbox Cool Hat

The best thing about a summer hat is the shade you carry around with you. The worst thing about it is that hats are often too hot. Make yourself a cool hat. This one is a copy of the genuine Chinese original, which was woven from grass. It is also cool to wear because head heat can escape through the holes. *You'll need:* cardboard (the large panels from big soapboxes are good), string or raffia, a large needle that will take string or raffia, scissors heavy enough to cut the cardboard, a nail for punching holes, a ruler and a pencil, and poster colors.

Measure and cut five cardboard triangles like the one shown in the drawing—about the same size (larger for big heads, smaller for babies). If you have a very large soapbox, you'll get two pieces from each large panel. Cut out the pieces.

Punch holes along the sides with the nail. Keep the spaces even. One hole per inch is good.

Lace the pieces together with string or raffia the same way you tie up your sneakers. Punch another hole on each side at the bottom for chin strings.

Now paint it up. The brighter the better.

If a mosquito bites you, you'll know it's a female because only *she* needs blood for her developing eggs. The male mosquito is satisfied by sucking on plants.

You could have a timekeeping garden. Flower clocks were popular in formal gardens in Europe. The opening and closing times of certain varieties of flower are very regular and exact; these flowers are planted in order in a ring, to make a "clock." Evening primroses, for example, open at 6:00 P.M.; African marigolds open at 7:00 A.M.

Novas are dying stars that suddenly become very big and bright. Supernovas are so bright that they can be seen in the daytime.

Less than 1 percent of the energy of the sun reaches the earth, but that is more than enough to meet the earth's needs. Many people are finding ways to use that energy; solar energy can heat our homes, provide hot water, and make electricity to do many other kinds of work.

The shell of a snapping turtle isn't the turtle's only defense. The turtle also depends on the quick movement of its snakelike neck and the sharpness and strength of its heavy jaws for defense and food gathering.

Some insects are such great helpers that gardeners buy them by the boxful and release them in the garden. Ladybugs, praying mantises, and lacewings are some of the bugs welcomed by gardeners.

Our language contains some old and wonderful words to name animal groups. You've probably heard of a herd of cows, but have you heard these old-fashioned terms: a gam of whales, a grist of bees, a leap of leopards, a knot of toads, a cast of hawks, a mob of kangaroos, a murder of crows?

	Monday June 13
	Tuesday June 14
	Wednesday June 15
	Thursday June 16
First Quarter Moon ◑	**Friday June 17**
	Saturday June 18
	Sunday June 19

Water Play

The best way to keep cool on a hot summer day is to get good and wet. You don't need a swimming place to have fun with water. You can still have a great time and get soaking wet if you have a garden hose and a patch of grass. Here are some ideas. So go put on your bathing suit.

Water Whip

Here is a wild water toy you can set up almost anywhere. When you turn on the faucet, it takes on a life of its own, thrashing about and throwing a stream of water in every direction. *You'll need:* a garden hose long enough to reach an outdoor faucet, some twine or rags for ties, a stake (an old broom handle is perfect), and a plastic nozzle for the hose. Don't use the metal kind because they are too heavy, and, besides, they hurt if you get bumped.

Drive the stake into a grassy place. You may need to get adult help for the stake. Use the rags or twine to tie the hose to the stake as shown. Be sure to leave about two feet of hose free. Turn the water on. Adjust the length of hose and the water pressure until your hose starts to behave like a wild animal. Then get wet!

stake
twine
hose

Water Slide

Water slides are wonderful, and guaranteed to keep you cool, even on the hottest days, while you run and skid and have a good old time. You should approach the water slide with some respect. It's also possible to slip and give your head a nasty crack on the ground.

You'll need: a length of plastic, at least ten feet long, but longer if possible, and a hose and sprinkler to keep it all wet. Find a grassy place where you can put the plastic, with extra room for a runway.

A plastic tarp about 20 by 20 feet costs around a dollar at the hardware or paint store. These are thin plastic and rip easily. It is better to buy about six yards of heavier plastic (called Visqueen). It will cost more, but will last many summers.

Set the plastic on the lawn where there are no lumps and bumps. Secure the corners with smooth stones or objects that won't scratch if you crash into them.

Set the sprinkler so that it keeps the surface wet and slick. Get a good run for it, then when your feet are on the plastic, see how far you can slide.

Pick up the plastic when you're finished. It isn't very good for the grass underneath.

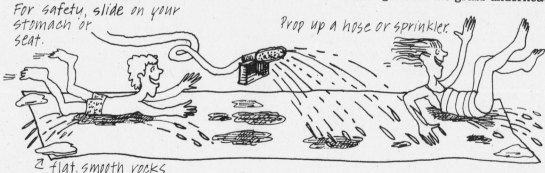

For safety, slide on your stomach or seat.

Prop up a hose or sprinkler.

flat, smooth rocks

Cucumbers are one of the more difficult vegetables to grow. They need lots of good soil, moisture, and attention. They are members of the gourd family, and so are relatives of melons, squashes, and pumpkins. Some varieties of cucumber are grown because they make good pickles.

Add some fancy words to your vocabulary. The turtle's shell is called the "carapace." The part beneath the turtle's body is attached to the carapace; it is called the "plastron."

Where there is no atmosphere, there is no weather. The patterns of weather are masses of air being heated, mixed, and moved about by the sun's energy.

Plants have families, just like people do. Usually the shape of a plant's flower tells which family it belongs to. Did you know that bell peppers, potatoes, tomatoes, and eggplants are all in the same family? It's the nightshade family.

A starfish that has lost an arm can slowly grow it back.

The "warts" on a toad are actually groups of glands that ooze a gummy white fluid when the toad is seized by a larger animal. All amphibians have this characteristic, but toads have it more than the rest. The fluid is very irritating to the mouths of other animals and teaches most of them the lesson "Don't eat toads." You can rest assured that the fluid does not cause warts.

A skunk will roll a toad in the grass to wipe away the poisons the toad oozes from its skin. In the same way the skunk will prepare for a meal of hairy caterpillar.

	Monday June 20
Summer Solstice	Tuesday June 21
	Wednesday June 22
	Thursday June 23
	Friday June 24
Partial Lunar Eclipse 3:22 A.M. Full Moon ○	Saturday June 25
	Sunday June 26

Monday June 27	
Tuesday June 28	
Wednesday June 29	
Thursday June 30	
Friday July 1 *Dominion Day (Canada)*	
Saturday July 2	
Sunday July 3 Last Quarter Moon	

Lizard tails break off easily. Often a predator grabbing a lizard ends up with a mouthful of tail, while the lizard scurries away.

There's a certain type of orchid whose flower looks just like the female of a certain type of fly. This look-alike stirs the interest of the male fly, who approaches and pollinates the flower while he's being fooled.

More names for animal groups are: a muster of peacocks, a pride of lions, a skulk of foxes, a span of mules, a trip of goats, a brace of ducks, a pod of seals, a sounder of boars.

The earliest humans got their food by killing animals and gathering wild plants. Little by little, though, they learned that the plants made seeds, which people could plant where they wanted them to grow. Every modern garden plant has a wild ancestor.

A broken worm might grow into a whole new worm. With its power of regeneration, this animal can grow new parts.

Water Hand

AN OLD, HEAVY RUBBER GLOVE

HOSE CLAMP

PUNCH HOLES.

GARDEN HOSE (TURN IT ON SLOWLY.)

Fasten a heavy rubber glove on the end of a garden hose. Use a metal hose clamp. Turn on the water a little. Punch very small holes in the end of each finger. Adjust the pressure so the fingers squirt.

Popsicles,
bananas, bombes & fruit cubes

OR There Is Nothing Quite So Nice As Ice

When the afternoon heat arrives and you are sure you won't live the rest of the day, it's time for some ice! If you've done a little advance preparation, you can slither onto a lawn chair with your favorite form of icicle and, until the dream melts away, pretend you're in an igloo in the far, far north. Here are our best ideas for cooler-downers.

Icy Treats

Juicy cubes. Freeze lemonade or fruit juice in an ice cube tray. When it's frozen, toss two or three cubes into a glass of sparkling ginger ale. Hoo ha!

Canned fruit slush. Here's what to do with the juice from a can of peaches or other fruit. Pour it into a shallow container (such as an ice cube tray without the dividers). Allow it to freeze a little. When it is beginning to turn solid, break it into chunks and toss them into the blender. Whip them up into an icy froth. Serve in an icy glass with a straw.

Cold Bananas

Bet you can't eat just one! To make six cold banana pops *you'll need:* three bananas, a small pack of chopped nuts, a 12-ounce package of chocolate chips, six wooden skewers for handles, some waxed paper, and 1½ tablespoons of vegetable oil. Plus you'll need an empty 6-ounce frozen juice can.

1. Peel the bananas and cut them in half crosswise. Stick a skewer in the flat end of each piece and freeze them on individual pieces of waxed paper.

2. When the bananas have been in the freezer for about 30 minutes, start the chocolate sauce. Fill a small saucepan half full of water and heat it on medium. Fill the juice can with half the package of chocolate chips (¾ cup) plus 1½ tablespoons of vegetable oil. When the water is hot, set the can of chips into the hot water so the chocolate will melt.

3. One at a time, take the banana pieces out of the freezer and dip them into the hot chocolate. Give each banana a turn as you pull it out of the hot liquid. While it's still wet, give each one a roll in the chopped nuts. Wrap each pop in a sheet of waxed paper and put it back into the freezer for another hour.

← filling lid

← scooped-out orange

Orange Bombe

Cut a hat-shaped section off the top of an orange. Scoop out the insides, and put the juice and pulp into a small bowl. Scrape the fruit pulp off the section membranes so you end up with just fruit. Add a couple of tablespoons of plain or flavored yogurt or soft vanilla ice cream and stir well. Now spoon the mixture back into the orange shell, replace its hat, and put it into the freezer for an hour. When it's ready, you'll have a frozen orange treat in its own icy cup. Eat it with a spoon.

waxed paper

skewer → ← half banana

melted chocolate →

metal juice can

sauce pan with water →

Roll in nuts.

Monday July 4 *Independence Day*	Not just bees and other insects serve as plant pollinators. Birds do this job too. Doves pollinate the saguaro, a cactuslike tree of our southwestern deserts. Hummingbirds pollinate many plants in home gardens. 
Tuesday July 5	 The shimmering rainbow colors of soap bubbles and some hummingbirds and beetles are called "iridescence." Iridescent things have several layers that reflect light; most things have one layer of pigment, and it reflects one solid color.
Wednesday July 6	A cow must eat more than 21 pounds of grain in order to produce 1 pound of steak. More people can be fed by the grain produced on an acre of land than by the steak that much land will produce.
Thursday July 7	*In most plants the growing goes on at the tip of the plant's shoots. When the tops of such plants are cut off, it takes a long time for the plants to recover. In grass plants, however, the growing goes on at the base. So when the top is eaten or cut, the plant keeps right on growing.*
Friday July 8	When the wind is in the south It blows the bait into fish's mouth. 
Saturday July 9	Thunder rumbles if it is fairly far away from you, but claps if it's very close. This is because the faraway sounds reach your ears at slightly different times, while the close ones boom in your ears all at once.
Sunday July 10 New Moon ●	It's not correct to say that bats navigate with radar. The electronic waves of radar behave differently from the sound waves that keep bats from crashing. Their method of making high-pitched squeaks and responding to their echoes is like the human invention called "sonar."

Some night-blooming plants are pollinated by bats. Such plants have developed special features to help make pollination possible. These plants must have strong stems, which can support the bat's weight, and long stems that are away from other foliage so the bat can find them easily with sonar.

The starfish is no ordinary eater. It pushes its stomach out through its mouth. The stomach surrounds the prey and digests it outside the starfish's body.

The highest temperature ever recorded in the United States was at Death Valley, California, in July 1913: 134° F. The coldest was at Prospect Creek, Alaska, in 1971: -80° F. The world's record for cold makes that seem balmy, though. Soviet scientists stationed on Antarctica measured -126° F. in 1960.

Reptiles use their tongues the way we use our noses. The reptile's tongue collects particles from the air on the surface of objects and passes them by an organ in the roof of its mouth. The organ identifies the particles by their smell.

The hummingbird's hum is made by its wings beating as fast as 70 times per second. This bird is so light — one-tenth of an ounce — that it can perch on a stem of grass. It doesn't need to perch on a flower petal, though, to drink flower nectar; it can hover in mid-air.

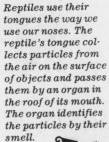

To be official, a temperature measurement must be made on instruments in a sheltered, ventilated location.

The kangaroo rat has adapted to survival in dry deserts, where it may often find only dry foods to eat. It has the ability to manufacture water from its food and to sweat away or excrete much less water than other animals do.

	Monday July 11
	Tuesday July 12
	Wednesday July 13
	Thursday July 14
	Friday July 15
First Quarter Moon ◑	**Saturday July 16**
	Sunday July 17

Monday July 18	
Tuesday July 19	
Wednesday July 20	
Thursday July 21	
Friday July 22	
Saturday July 23	
Sunday July 24 Full Moon ○	

With its long sticky tongue a toad can catch and swallow as many as 300 insects during a warm summer night. The tongue is attached at the front, not the rear, of its mouth. This helps make those lightning flicks possible. With such a weapon it doesn't need to get close to its prey.

The world's oceans contain enough salt to cover the United States with a salt layer 1½ inches deep.

Corn is the only member of the grass family which we can use as a fresh vegetable. All the rest are grains and must be cooked for a fairly long time before they are eaten.

The jawfish protects itself by digging a hole in the ocean floor and hiding there. The male jawfish holds the female's eggs in his wide mouth, usually for three or four days, until they hatch. When he eats or digs, he spits out the eggs first, then soon scoops them up again.

There are four kinds of poisonous snakes in the United States. They are the coral snake, the rattle-snake, the cotton-mouth water moccasin, and the copperhead.

Nothing can travel faster than light. Light flashes faster than 186,000 miles per second. The sun is about 93,000,000 miles from the earth. That means that light leaving the sun takes about eight minutes to reach your eyes.

The Polyphemus moth needs a certain chemical in order to mate, and the red oak produces that chemical. The female moth can't fly to find her mate, so she relies on the "perfume" the tree makes to attract him to her.

MONSTERBUG

How to Build the Biggest Insect Ever

You are surrounded by buzzing, fluttering, crawling friends. A closer look will tell you that they are both complex and beautiful. Use a magnifier to look at some of these creatures. How many kinds of parts can you identify?

Bug parts look the way they do for a reason. Each is designed to do a special

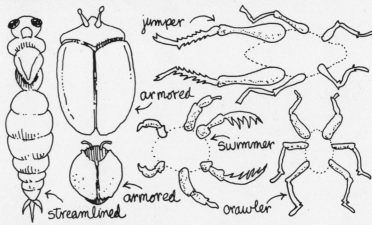

task. A soft and fuzzy wing is used for fluttering, while a lacy, clear wing is more for buzzing. Some wings are hidden under a protective shell, for emergency use only.

Bug body parts can be streamlined for flying, or round and armor plated for a defensive life on the ground. A bug's leg will tell you whether its owner crawls, glides on the water, or leaps through the air. You can mix and match all these parts, and create a Monsterbug of your own!

(continued on page 47)

Monday July 25	
Tuesday July 26	
Wednesday July 27	
Thursday July 28	
Friday July 29	
Saturday July 30	
Sunday July 31	

Some vegetables are plant parts that don't contain the plant's seeds. Carrots, beets, and turnips are fat roots. Lettuce, chard, and cabbage are leaves. Asparagus is a stem. Artichoke and broccoli are flowers that haven't opened yet.

Here's how to tell if a spotted skunk is about to spray. It does a handstand; and with its hindquarters and tail straight up, it looks backwards through its front legs at whatever is threatening. The stinky spray causes a burning sensation on skin and can produce temporary and very painful blindness if it lands in the eyes of human or beast.

The nearest star is so far away that its light takes more than four years to reach us.

SMOKEY SAYS

PREVENT FOREST FIRES!

How do rangers decide when to close forests because of fire danger? Mainly they use a device made of a few sticks of wood. When the weight of the sticks drops below a certain level, it means that there's very little moisture in the air—the perfect condition for a fire to spread fast.

Days and nights at the equator are always 12 hours long. During summer in the far north, the sun shines across the pole of the earth and so does not set. To an observer in this "land of the midnight sun," the sun appears to move along the horizon instead of rising and setting.

Located between each eye and nostril of the rattlesnake is a "pit organ," which senses slight changes in temperature. The pit organs enable the snake to judge the location and distance of a warm-blooded creature, and so, when to strike at its prey. Even without its other senses, the snake could survive with the use of this uncommon organ.

Bald-faced hornets beat their wings to fan their nests on hot days. If this fanning doesn't cool the nests enough, they will fly to a mudhole or pond, then fly back and dump mouthfuls of liquid on the outside of the nest. Evaporation of water takes heat out of the nests.

A rattlesnake's fangs aren't permanent, but are replaced by new ones every so often. If the snake had to wait for a new fang to grow in every time one was lost, there would often be times when it had neither protection nor the power to kill its food. On each side of its upper jaw there are two fang sockets. A new fang is always growing in one socket on each side, ready to swing into active position when it is needed.

Meteors are chunks made up mostly of nickel and iron. We can see meteors when they enter our atmosphere and run into enough oxygen to begin burning brightly. The bright streaks they make in the sky give them the nickname "shooting stars."

A Noisy Picture

Can you *see* four noises in this illustration?

Last Quarter Moon	**Monday August 1**
	Tuesday August 2
	Wednesday August 3
	Thursday August 4
	Friday August 5
	Saturday August 6
	Sunday August 7

Monday August 8	New Moon ●
Tuesday August 9	
Wednesday August 10	
Thursday August 11	
Friday August 12	
Saturday August 13	
Sunday August 14	

Most nuts grow on trees, but peanuts grow underground. The peanut plant is short and bushy above the ground, and forms its seed pods—peanuts—in the soil.

The African crocodile lets the crocodile bird enter its wide open mouth to pick worms and insects from among its sharp teeth.

Not all of the sun's rays are good for us. One type of solar radiation—ultraviolet light—can kill cells in our bodies. A layer of a gas high in the earth's atmosphere called "ozone" blocks out most ultraviolet rays. Skin protects us from the rays that get through the ozone; tanning is the body's way of protecting us from ultraviolet rays.

Wheat fields take up more land than any other food crop in the world.

Evening primroses open their flowers when the temperature drops at the end of the day. One type cannot open at all, no matter how cool the evening is, unless the daytime temperature reached about 68° F. The warmer the day has been, the more rapidly the flower opens.

When it is born, a giraffe calf is almost as tall as a full-grown human.

Meteors usually burn up completely before they reach the earth's surface, but once in a while one hits. Meteor Crater is a very big hole where a meteor struck the ground in the Arizona desert thousands of years ago.

Monsterbug, *the biggest insect ever!*

(continued from page 43)

Here is how. All insects are made from a basic group of body parts. Sort of like a kit. Some are for hopping around, some for swimming or crawling. Some of those parts are drawn on the grid at the right. Make a grid of one-inch squares on a big sheet of cardboard or wrapping paper. Then copy the body parts as they are drawn, making sure that each big square looks like each little one, as shown below. If you are drawing on cardboard, you can cut out the parts right away and decorate them. If you use paper for the big grid, use the paper parts as patterns. Cut out each pattern part and transfer the design to heavier material. Invent a Monsterbug. You can make jumping flyers, or swimming crawlers. Big ones. Combine different parts from your Monsterbug kit.

(For assembly instructions, see page 50.)

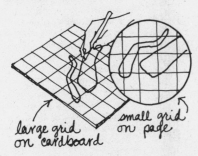

large grid on cardboard

small grid on page

Monday August 15	**First Quarter Moon** ◑
Tuesday August 16	
Wednesday August 17	
Thursday August 18	
Friday August 19	
Saturday August 20	
Sunday August 21	

Astronomers have learned that meteors are more likely to sail into view at certain seasons of the year than at others. Enough meteors may appear at the same time to be called "meteor showers."

Insect-eating bats don't catch their prey directly with their mouths. The large membranes which stretch between their wings are used as scoop nets. These enfold insects and bring them within reach of the bat's jaws.

Crocodiles look like they're protected by a kind of armor — their tough hide — but they can't stay out in the blazing sun for long. Exposure for less than an hour can sometimes be fatal. They need to go into water often to lower their body temperature. Smearing mud all over themselves also helps. The frightening, wide-open jaws are letting out heat.

The noise inside a seashell may sound like the ocean, but it isn't. Normal sounds around you are echoing back and forth inside the shell, and the spiral shape makes those sounds louder.

There's a "fast-gun" orchid with a trigger device that shoots sticky pollen at nearby bees.

When evening comes, one underwater plant lifts a special "door" above the surface to admit a particular species of beetle. Then, with the door shut, the beetle spends the whole night in a waterproof room lapping up nectar and pollinating the plant. In the morning the door rises and the beetle checks out.

The sun is a star. It is by far the biggest, brightest star in our skies because it is so much closer than any other star. Compared to other stars, though, it is about average in size, brightness, and temperature.

We can be fairly sure that a "water crisis" will occur in many places fairly soon. This may affect people as much as the "energy crisis" has. When we realize that it takes 10,000 gallons of water to grow a bushel of corn and 65,000 gallons to make a ton of steel, it seems that icebergs could be an important water source for the future.

Birds of prey include hawks, eagles, and falcons. They survive by killing mice, snakes, and other small animals. Small birds are sometimes on the menu of birds of prey. The hunter plucks the feathers from the prey before eating it.

Lack of rainfall ruins many crops. Most crops need at least 20 inches during their growing time. Where little or no rain falls, crops can be grown very well by "irrigation," which is watering them with water stored in ponds, lakes, rivers, or underground.

The heat from a fire is needed to force some kinds of seeds to sprout. Forest fires burn down some plants, but cause others to start growing.

The rate at which katydids produce their calls is related to how active the insect's body is, and their body activity is controlled by the air temperature. So it's possible to figure out the temperature by counting the calls: add 161 to the number of calls in a minute, then divide by 3 to get the temperature in Fahrenheit.

Monday August 22

Full Moon
○

Tuesday August 23

Wednesday August 24

Thursday August 25

Friday August 26

Saturday August 27

Sunday August 28

Monsterbug, the biggest insect ever!

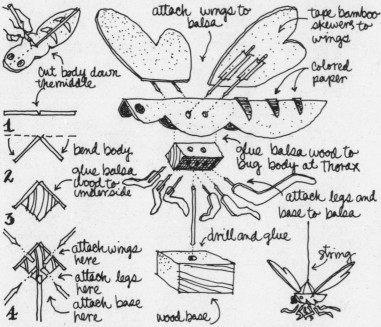

attach wings to balsa

tape bamboo skewers to wings

Colored paper

Cut body down the middle

1

bend body.

2

glue balsa wood to underside

3

glue balsa wood to bug body at thorax

attach legs and base to balsa

attach wings here

attach legs here

attach base here

4

drill and glue

wood base

string

at one end) to the underside of each leg and wing. Then you can attach the legs and wings to the body by poking the sharp stick ends into the balsa-wood block, as shown. Hang your Monsterbug by a string, or mount it on a base, as shown in the drawing at the left.

You can also attach insect "accessories" to your Monsterbug by taping them to the bug body. These might be antennae, bug eyes, big crusher jaws, mouth suction tubes, fuzzy tails, pincers, and long scary stingers. Choose the best one for your custom Monsterbug.

(continued from page 47)
Assemble your Monsterbug parts and display your creation on the wall or the tabletop, or hang it from the ceiling. The easiest way to add color to your Monsterbug is to cut the parts out of colored mat board, which comes in many colors and can be purchased at an art supply or framing shop. Or you can glue colored paper onto the bug parts, or you can paint them and stick on colored "dot" labels, available at stationery stores. Insects have lots of color, so

use your imagination. If you are stuck for ideas, look at a real bug.

Using an x-acto knife, cut down the center of the middle body section, which is the "thorax." (All insects have a head, thorax, and abdomen. The wings and legs are attached to the thorax.) Be sure not to cut it all the way through, but just enough so it will bend neatly, as shown above. Glue a balsa-wood block to the thorax. Then tape or glue a thin stick (bamboo skewers work well and are pointed

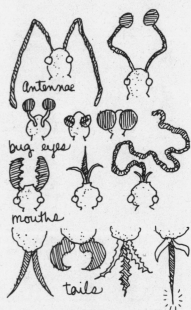

antennae

bug eyes

mouths

tails

We live at the bottom of an ocean of air called the "atmosphere." This "ocean" is about 1,000 miles deep. Only the lightest gases—hydrogen and helium—are found at this ocean's top. The air where we are is much denser and heavier; most of the weight of the atmosphere lies in the bottom 3½ miles.

Small birds recognize a hawk's shape, or silhouette, as it passes overhead. To prove this, scientists passed cardboard shapes resembling a hawk's silhouette over some birds, and they scurried away. The birds did *not* react to the silhouettes of birds that do not hunt them.

Sweet corn is a favorite food, but it's truly delicious only if it's eaten soon after it has been picked. Once the corn has been picked, the sugar in it begins to turn to starch; within two days it is no longer sweet.

This may be confusing! When English people say "corn," they mean what we Americans call "wheat." By "corn," the Scotch mean "oats." What we call "corn" others call "maize."

The temperature of the sun on its surface is about 10,000° F. Inside this blazing star, temperatures reach 35,000° F.

Porcupines don't shoot their quills. A threatened porcupine will strike these barbs directly into an enemy by slapping with its tail or shoving with its body. A porcupine is very slow moving, but it can lash out quickly.

Monday August 29

Tuesday August 30

Last Quarter Moon

Wednesday August 31

Thursday September 1

Friday September 2

Saturday September 3

Sunday September 4

some hints on
How to Draw Animals

Do you have sharp eyes? Good, because they're the most important tools you need to draw animals. Or anything else. Sharp eyes and lots of paper. The rest is practice. Lots of it. The best thing about drawing is that the more you do, the more fun it is. So sharpen your eyes, collect lots of paper and a soft pencil, and you're ready to start.

Looking at the Cat

1. Begin with an animal you know well, like your own cat or dog. Or borrow one from a neighbor or a zoo. Pick a time when the animal is resting. Now you need those eyes. Put yourself in a comfortable place and look hard. Start by looking at the biggest shapes. Is a sleeping cat shaped something like an egg? Not quite. So just drawing an egg won't do. Open your eyes wide to see what the biggest shapes are and how they are arranged.

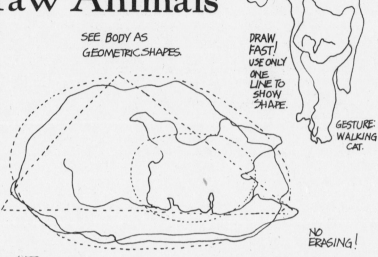

SEE BODY AS GEOMETRIC SHAPES.

DRAW FAST! USE ONLY ONE LINE TO SHOW SHAPE.

GESTURE: WALKING CAT.

NO ERASING!

GESTURE: CLOSE-UP. REMEMBER, NO DETAIL IN GESTURE DRAWINGS.

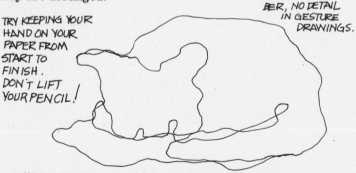

TRY KEEPING YOUR HAND ON YOUR PAPER FROM START TO FINISH. DON'T LIFT YOUR PENCIL!

GESTURE DRAWING: SLEEPING CAT. DO LOTS AND LOTS OF THESE FAST SIMPLE DRAWINGS.

2. Draw only a few lines to make the main shapes. Don't fiddle with it or try to erase. If you don't like the first one, do another. In fact, do more even if you do like the first one. This kind of fast main-shape drawing is called "gesture drawing." That's how your hand gets acquainted with what your eye is seeing. If you remember how many times you practiced making letters before you could write your name, you'll have some idea of how many cat gestures you need to make.

Stop and Think

Stop once in a while to look at the drawings. Which looks most like a sleeping cat? Why does it? Keep looking and drawing.

(continued on page 57)

John Burroughs called September "the month of tall weeds." Ralph Waldo Emerson wrote, "A weed is a plant whose virtues have not yet been discovered."

Which animal is the fastest? That's hard to measure exactly, but here's a rough idea. These numbers are expressed in miles per hour, but they give the top speed the animal could keep up for only one-quarter mile: cheetah, 70; pronghorn, 61; lion, 50; coyote, 43; zebra, 40; giraffe, 32; grizzly bear, 30; cat, 30; human, 27; elephant, 25; spider, 1; snail, .03.

The grasshopper's ears are located in its front knees, and work in much the same way as a human's ears. Honeybees are deaf.

You can tell what a bird eats and where it lives just by looking at its mouth and feet. Seed eaters have heavy bills for cracking seeds; meat eaters have strong, hooked bills for tearing meat. Swimming birds have webbed feet; marsh birds have long, trim toes to keep them from sinking in the mud.

Certain weeds are so common in our country that they seem "American," but many of them, like the Pilgrims and early settlers, traveled here from Europe. Some of them are: dandelion, nettle, thistle, pigweed, plantain, mallow, wild mustard, and wild radish.

The alligator snapping turtle of the lower Mississippi and Gulf states is a skillful fisherman who uses "bait." The turtle sits still and partly hidden on a muddy river bottom. Within its open jaws floats a pinkish sliver of flesh, which a passing fish believes is a wriggling worm. To get it, the fish must enter the jaws. Snap!

Monday September 5
Labor Day

Tuesday September 6
New Moon
●

Wednesday September 7

Thursday September 8
*Eve of Jewish New Year
Rosh Hashanah*

Friday September 9

Saturday September 10

Sunday September 11

Monday September 12	
Tuesday September 13 First Quarter Moon ◗	
Wednesday September 14	
Thursday September 15	
Friday September 16	
Saturday September 17 *Eve of Jewish Day of Atonement Yom Kippur*	
Sunday September 18	

The planet that looks and seems most like Earth is Venus; it is the planet closest to ours, is about the same size, and has storms of clouds swirling around it, just like Earth does. But the atmosphere of Venus would be deadly to us. It is full of carbon dioxide and sulfuric acid, which are poisonous for us to breathe. Also, at Venus' surface, winds blow 200 miles per hour, and the temperature is 900° F.

None of these South American animals has a hump, but they all belong to the same family as the camel: guanacos and vicunas are wild, llamas and alpacas are domesticated — they live with people.

Cucumbers, squash, peas, and tomatoes are all fruits, just as much as melons, cherries, grapes, and bananas are. All fruits are fleshy and have seeds inside, which describes some of the foods we think of as vegetables.

One South American termite queen produced over 70,000 eggs in a single day. It has been estimated that a single termite colony contained 3,000,000 individuals, all of them the offspring of a single queen.

Some seed coats are so waterproof that they can be soaked for months, or even years, without letting water reach the seed inside. Coconuts float for long periods of time and don't germinate until they reach land. This explains why there are coconut palm trees found on thousands of separate islands around the world.

The water scorpion has a snorkel. It can breathe air through this tube while remaining an inch or more below the surface of the water. The tube is also jointed so that the scorpion can move about.

The least bittern lives around swamps and protects itself by imitating the narrow grasses and cattail reeds that grow there. The bird can pull in its body so that it looks amazingly thin. Audubon, the famous bird painter and scientist, showed that the least bittern could pass between two books set only one inch apart, without moving them.

Potatoes are an important food because they can be easily stored for cooking later on. Potato leaves are poisonous; and for a long time this fact caused people to be afraid to eat the potato tuber, which is delicious baked, mashed, or fried.

The flying lizard can't really fly, but it can glide as far as 50 feet. To help it do this, the lizard has folds of skin along its body, which spread out when it spreads its legs wide.

The full moon that happens nearest to the autumn equinox is called the "harvest" moon. A full moon rises at sunset, and in the fall gives farmers some extra hours of light by which to harvest crops before frost and winter come.

Elephant Pie

Simply by rearranging the pieces of this pie, you can make the elephant run. Can you do it?

Monday September 19

Tuesday September 20

Wednesday September 21

Full Moon ○   **Thursday September 22**

Autumn Equinox   **Friday September 23**

Saturday September 24

Sunday September 25

Monday September 26	
Tuesday September 27	
Wednesday September 28	
Thursday September 29 Last Quarter Moon ◖	
Friday September 30	
Saturday October 1	
Sunday October 2	

As September draws to a close, the call of the katydid gets shorter, like the days. "Katy-did-it" dwindles to "katy-did," then to "katy," and finally to a cold, hoarse "kate."

Many kinds of monkeys spend several hours a day picking dirt and insects from each other's fur. This activity is called "grooming."

One year a late freeze damaged thousands of nut-bearing trees in the South. In the fall millions of squirrels in North Carolina, Tennessee, Georgia, and Mississippi discovered that there were hardly any nuts for them to gather and store. Frantically the squirrels began to travel toward any place where they might find nuts, even swimming rivers and lakes.

Insects are "cold-blooded," which means their body temperature is close to the temperature of the air around them. They have difficulty on cool days; then they must do a kind of warming-up exercise of flexing their wings before they can take off.

There are two basic types of clouds: cumulus clouds look piled-up and puffy; stratus clouds appear in sheets or thin, foglike layers. Height, temperature, and other factors create many cloud types related to these two.

Neptune was discovered because scientists knew something had to be causing Uranus to "wobble" in its orbit. When the orbits of these two planets come fairly close, they tug on each other through the effect of gravity.

More Hints on How to Draw Animals

(*continued from page 52*)

3. When you have made lots of gesture drawings, you can begin to add detail. Start with your best gesture drawing and add to it. Look at the individual shapes of legs, paws, ears, and face. What shapes are they? Try to see how one part connects to another. Work simply and fast. Try to get all the shapes now, but don't be too fussy. When you have a drawing you like, then you can think about adding color.

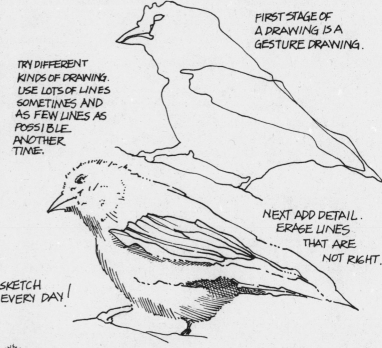

TRY DIFFERENT KINDS OF DRAWING. USE LOTS OF LINES SOMETIMES AND AS FEW LINES AS POSSIBLE. ANOTHER TIME.

FIRST STAGE OF A DRAWING IS A GESTURE DRAWING.

NEXT ADD DETAIL. ERASE LINES THAT ARE NOT RIGHT.

SKETCH EVERY DAY!

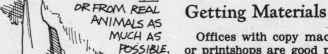

DRAW FROM *LIFE* OR FROM REAL ANIMALS AS MUCH AS POSSIBLE.

Other Hints

When your hand has learned the cat, try other subjects. If the animal is awake, and moving, you need to work very fast and your eyes need to be sharp. Look at your drawings often as you work to see which one is best and why. If you know why you like one better than another, you will be able to repeat it the next time. Save your money for a little blank book you can carry around with you for sketching. Sketch something every day. Your hand is a good learner, but you have to keep it busy or it forgets.

Getting Materials

Offices with copy machines or printshops are good places to get free waste paper. For practice it doesn't matter if there is printing on the back of your drawing. Printshops also have *trims,* usually in smaller sheets. This is often good paper, and sometimes you can get it for nothing. Newspapers have the unprinted ends of newsprint rolls. For pencil work, use a number 1 or an F lead. Those are soft leads that make nice, dark lines. You can also use felt-tipped pens, but they're more expensive.

LIRPA LOOF!
How Many Things Can You Find Wrong Here

The ruby-throated hummingbird migrates 2,000 miles every spring and fall. Its route takes it directly across the Gulf of Mexico, 500 miles of continuous flying for this tiny wonder.

Some plants and animals are more sensitive to chemicals than humans are, and they're often used as a way of detecting those chemicals. The cattleya orchid responds quickly to very small amounts of poisonous ethylene gas. Miners used to use canaries to tell if there was enough oxygen in the mines to breathe.

Some astronomers believe Pluto is an escaped satellite of Neptune. They suggest that it was once the third and farthest moon from Neptune and that somehow it broke away. It is so far away that from Pluto the sun would seem to be just another star in the sky.

Some plants live for only a part of one year. These are called "annuals." Some plants live into a second year before they make seeds and die. These are "biennials." Plants that live for many years are called "perennials."

A jack rabbit is called that for its long, upstanding ears, like those of a jackass. With its long, strong legs, it takes high flying leaps, like a kangaroo.

Goldfish are a variety of carp, a fish that grows to about a foot long. Wild carp have plain colors that help them to hide. People have bred goldfish to develop the color that gives them their name.

Monday October 3

Tuesday October 4

Wednesday October 5

New Moon ● Thursday October 6

Friday October 7

Saturday October 8

Sunday October 9

Monday October 10

Columbus Day

Tuesday October 11

Wednesday October 12

Thursday October 13

First Quarter Moon

Friday October 14

Saturday October 15

Sunday October 16

There seem to be no definite rules about how leaves change their colors in autumn. Each year they're liable to change to a slightly different shade. When summer has been particularly hot or winds have been strong enough to injure a tree, its foliage generally turns earlier and takes on a deeper shade.

What's the difference between turtles and tortoises? Turtles have webbed feet, usually for swimming, but even land species such as the box turtle have this feature. Tortoises are almost helpless in water and have been known to drown. Their feet are club shaped and equipped with heavy claws for digging.

Mushrooms are very sensitive to gravity and will adjust themselves if they are upset from growing straight up. They need to stand up straight so that their spores can be released. If necessary to achieve this, a mushroom can even develop gills (the openings where spores come out) on its top.

The Arctic tern is the champion long-distance flier. On its migrations, twice a year, it travels 11,000 miles.

The walkingstick is an insect that looks just like a stick; its legs are twiglike. This imitation protects it from enemies, which often don't notice it. Color changes help it too. A newly hatched walkingstick is light green, matching the spring leaves. As weeks go by, it turns darker and darker until, by fall, it is the brown color of many autumn leaves.

When the white-tailed deer runs toward safety, it raises its tail and shows the white hair on the underside. Other deer that spot this white "flag" know that an enemy is near.

What animal is the strongest? (The snail —it carries its house.)

A turtle's lungs can't pump normally when it pulls into its shell. This is because its body is so tightly packed inside. Startled turtles often give out a short hiss, which is not a sign of fear or excitement, but the sound of breath being forced out to make room for the body parts. One way the turtle can get air into its lungs is by swallowing.

The next full moon after the harvest moon is known as the "hunter's" moon.

Earth's atmosphere is a mixture of quite a few gases. By far the main ingredient is nitrogen. Second comes oxygen, which we and all other animals must have in order to breathe. The rest of the atmosphere—about 1 percent—is argon, carbon dioxide, neon, helium, krypton, and xenon.

The Anableps (that's its Latin name) is a four-eyed fish that can see above and below water at the same time. The pupil of each of its two eyes is divided in half—that makes four eyes. Not surprisingly, this fish eats both plants and insects it finds in the air and tiny fish it can spot in the water.

Night is a shadow. When our side of the earth is turned away from the bright sun, we are in the shadow that our planet makes. The earth is always casting a shadow, but we are in it only about half the time because of the earth's spinning.

During the short summers in the arctic region, musk oxen feed round-the-clock. They live off their fat during winter. The short legs of these animals present a problem when deep drifts of snow pile up. During a storm a herd of musk oxen gathers into a tight circle, with the adults all facing out and the young in the middle. If necessary, they'll stay on their feet for days, waiting out the storm.

Monday October 17

Tuesday October 18

Wednesday October 19

Thursday October 20

Full Moon
Friday October 21

Saturday October 22

Sunday October 23

Creature Features

Stockings make great masks. Not just for bank robbers, but for kids posing as creatures. The easiest kind to work with is the heavy stretch sort, such as tights. But any color or texture stocking will make a mask, although the effects will differ with different stockings. *You will need:* a single stocking for the fowl and the duck and a pair of panty hose or tights for the wabbit. You will also need stuffing, scissors, a felt marker, a rubber band, string, pins, broom straws, and 35-millimeter film cans. (Ask for these at your local film developer, who will be delighted to give them away.)

Weird Wabbit

① Clip off the feet.

② Knot each leg from the inside. Stuff the legs.

③ Put them on. Roll up a ball of stuffing for the nose. Fix it in place with a rubber band.

④ Cut out the eye and nose holes.

⑤ Pad the cheeks.

⑥ Add broom-straw whiskers.

Foul Fowl

① Put on a single stocking.

② Clip and knot the end.

③ Mark the eyes and nose.

④ Cut the holes.

⑤ Snap on some film cans.

Dumb Duck

① Test the stocking for fit.

② Stuff the leg and foot so it stands up straight.

③ Poke in pins for the eyes.

④ Tie off the bill.

⑤ To make a horse, tie off the ears and flatten the nose.

can
lid

pin
bead

hmmmnn...

DAD?

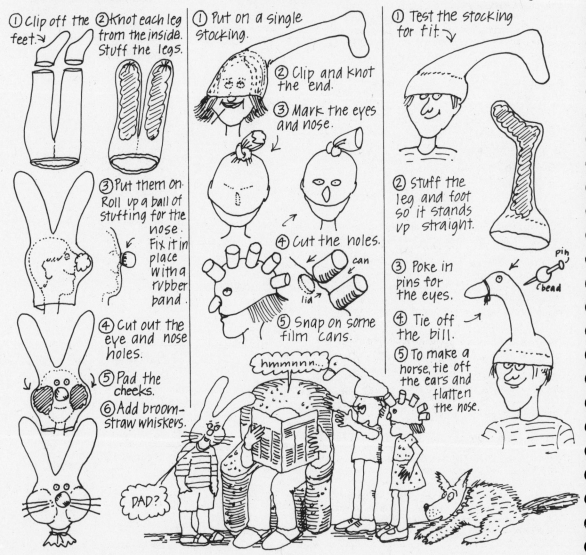

Soybeans are a great source of protein. That means that foods made from them can add to your diet what meat, fish, and eggs do. Most soybeans are fed to animals, but more and more of them are being used as food for people. Have you heard of tofu?

The chuckwalla is a large lizard whose home is in the rocky desert hills of the Southwest. When in danger, it slips into a narrow space between rocks and puffs itself up even bigger. This action wedges the chuckwalla in so tight that it can't be pulled out by an attacker.

Why did the fly fly? (Because the spider spied her.)

A telescope reveals that Mercury and Venus appear in phases; like the moon, they keep changing shape. We see the rest of the planets as full, except Mars, which sometimes is not quite full.

The Sargasso Sea is a sea completely surrounded by the Atlantic Ocean. It rotates in place, dragged round and round by a circular system of ocean currents. This strange place takes its name from sargassum, a long, branching seaweed that grows densely there. Most seaweeds are anchored to the ocean bottom or some other support, but sargassum just floats.

The male dance fly, while courting, captures a smaller insect, wraps it in silk spun from its own salivary glands, and presents it "gift-wrapped" to his favorite female.

'The deepest lake in the United States is Crater Lake in Oregon. The lake was formed when an ancient volcano erupted and exploded so totally that what was left just caved in, leaving an enormous pit. The pit gradually filled with rain water and melted snow; the lake is 1,932 feet deep.

Monday October 24

Tuesday October 25

Wednesday October 26

Make a weird mask for Halloween. See page 62.

Thursday October 27

Last Quarter Moon

Friday October 28

Saturday October 29

Sunday October 30

63

Feeders for Tiny Diners

(*continued from page 26*)

Tiny Diners. One of the best ways to get to know a bug is to have it over for a meal! Make some simple feeders that will let you get a close look at creatures who are normally in too big a hurry to stick around.

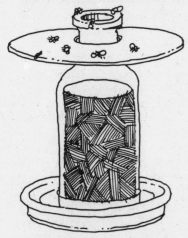

Ant apartment. You can study ants at home with a small ant farm. Fill a wide-mouthed bottle with damp sand and set it in a bowl of water. Cut a circle of cardboard with a hole in the middle large enough to go over the neck of the bottle. Feed the ants on this circular "terrace." Give them small amounts of honey, fruit, or peanut butter. To load the farm, gently scoop up as many ants as possible from a nest in your yard or at the park.

Bee feeder. Dine with several hundred bees on your windowsill with this simple feeder. Gently poke tiny holes in the lid of a glass jar, using a heavy needle (or a very small nail) and hammer. Then tape a bridle of string to the jar, as shown below, and fill the jar with honey or thick, well-mixed sugar water. Then hang the jar in front of a second-story window and watch who comes to eat with you.

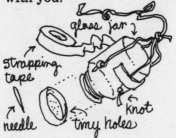

strapping tape

glass jar

needle

tiny holes

knot

Midnight snack. You can attract and observe many beautiful moths simply by giving them a nightly treat. Mix together either fruit pulp and sugar or brown sugar and beer. Tie a tennis ball to a length of string; and, on a warm night, dip it into the sticky, sweet stuff. Hang this treat from the top of a window. Within an hour you should have attracted some lovely, hungry visitors. Try hanging more than one ball—in different locations. Do you think you will attract the same kinds of moths in each location?

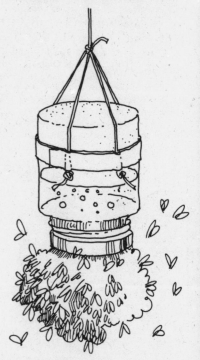

The word "pumpkin" comes from the French word *pompion,* which came from a Greek word meaning "cooked by the sun." The best pumpkins are those left to ripen in the sun.

Under a microscope you can see that the stinger of a honeybee has tiny barbs along its edges. These barbs point backward, so the stinger can easily pierce the skin, but not so easily pull out again. Often when a bee stings, it leaves its stinger in its victim. The loss of its stinger causes the death of the bee.

Other stars besides the sun may have planets orbiting around them, but they are so far away that it's hard to tell.

Weather systems normally move eastward 500 to 600 miles per day.

Here's an example of the balance of nature that man can undo. Sheep and cattle graze on grassy rangelands. Coyotes sometimes attack these defenseless animals, but they also eat mice and other rodents. Rodents eat grass seeds. Where people have wiped out coyotes with guns and traps, the population of rodents has increased tremendously. Much more grass seed is eaten by them on the rangelands, so less grass can sprout for cattle and sheep to eat.

Hurricanes always form over water in or near the tropical regions of the globe. Tornadoes spring up over land and have been reported on every continent and in every one of the United States.

How does the flying squirrel fly? It has long folds of skin along its sides from wrist to ankle. These stretch out when the squirrel spreads out its legs and act as a sail. A wide flat tail helps in steering. The flying squirrel's leaps through the air aren't really flying since they are always from a higher to a lower point.

Monday October 31
Halloween

Tuesday November 1

Wednesday November 2

Thursday November 3

New Moon
● Friday November 4

Saturday November 5

Sunday November 6

Monday November 7	*People in all countries of the world have agreed to measure time in the same way. This is done by dividing the globe into 24 time zones, each one hour of time apart. Some countries can't get along with each other, but at least they agree about what time it is!*
Tuesday November 8 *Election Day*	**The flying squirrel is extremely timid and shy. If it's handled roughly, instead of trying to escape, it's more likely to be paralyzed by fear and may die of shock.**
Wednesday November 9	The termite has very thin skin, which makes it very sensitive to dry air because moisture evaporates easily from its body. When termites are exposed to air that seems comfortable to us, they will soon shrivel up and die.
Thursday November 10	
Friday November 11 *Veterans Day*	## Zoo Puzzle Marcella, whose uncle is a zookeeper, has agreed to help her uncle feed the animals for a week. He has given her the diagram below, which takes her 18 turns from the time she leaves the feed barn until she returns with empty buckets. Marcella would like to figure out how to go to all 63 cages making *fewer* turns. Can you help her discover a new route?
Saturday November 12 First Quarter Moon ◐	
Sunday November 13	Hint: There are more than one!

Endangered species are animals and plants that are in danger of becoming extinct. Some endangered species living in North America are: American alligator, American crocodile, Eastern indigo snake, California condor, whooping crane, bald eagle, brown pelican, ivory-billed woodpecker, Columbian white-tailed deer, Virginia big-eared bat, jaguar, and margay.

Several types of insects that live in water have no way to use the oxygen supply in water. They must breathe air, so they must regularly come to the surface to get it. Back swimmers have hairs that catch little air bubbles, which stick to the insect as it swims below again.

Antarctica is a continent set in a partly frozen ocean. The Arctic is an ocean full of drifting ice, dotted with islands, and nearly ringed by continents. Antarctica is high above the surrounding sea; its average elevation is 6,000 feet above sea level, and it has peaks rising to 19,000 feet. There is much more life in the Arctic than on Antarctica.

Bananas do not grow on trees. The tropical plant which bears this fruit is really an herb. Instead of roots, it has rhizomes, which are underground stems. It has no trunk either, just leaves wrapped tightly in a tube shape.

Here are some endangered species from around the world: African elephant, red kangaroo, gray whale, black howler monkey, tiger, wild yak, West African ostrich, golden parakeet, and Australian parrot.

The horned toad is not a toad—it's a lizard. Its "horns" are a crown of spines that project from the back of its head and make it hard to swallow. It uses another defense to keep from being grabbed at all: it can shoot a fine spray of blood from its eye! The spray comes out quite hard and can travel several well-aimed feet.

Monday November 14

Tuesday November 15

Wednesday November 16

Thursday November 17

Friday November 18

Saturday November 19

Full Moon
○

Sunday November 20

Monday November 21	
Tuesday November 22	
Wednesday November 23	
Thursday November 24 *Thanksgiving Day*	
Friday November 25	
Saturday November 26	
Sunday November 27	Last Quarter Moon ◑

Seeds from the Arctic lupine, a wild-flower, were determined to have been frozen for 10,000 years. Would they still grow? Scientists reported that several sprouted and developed into healthy plants.

The legs of water striders don't poke through the water's surface. Under a microscope you can see thousands of short, tiny, slightly oily hairs on its legs and body. These keep the insect from getting wet and sinking. It's like floating a needle in a glass of water; the water molecules stick together to form a tough film on the surface.

There's a kind of marine alga that luminesces, or glows, at just about midnight every 24 hours. Even if it is grown in complete darkness, it continues to glow at its regular time.

A volcanic mountain on Mars, Olympus Mons, is 3 times higher than Earth's highest mountain, Mount Everest. Mars also has a grand canyon that makes the Grand Canyon in Arizona look like a scratch. The Valles Marineris is 4 miles deep and 3,000 miles long, 100 times as long as the Grand Canyon.

Koalas in dry regions of Australia get most of their water from the leaves of eucalyptus trees.

Every minute of every day hundreds of small earthquakes occur. They are so mild that they can be measured only by very sensitive instruments.

The humpback whale uses a net of bubbles to catch food. The whale dives far underwater and starts to blow bubbles as it swims in a circle. The bubbles rise to the surface. Very quickly the whale swims upward through the middle of the circle and eats the small fish that are trapped between the rising bubbles.

More Native American Toys

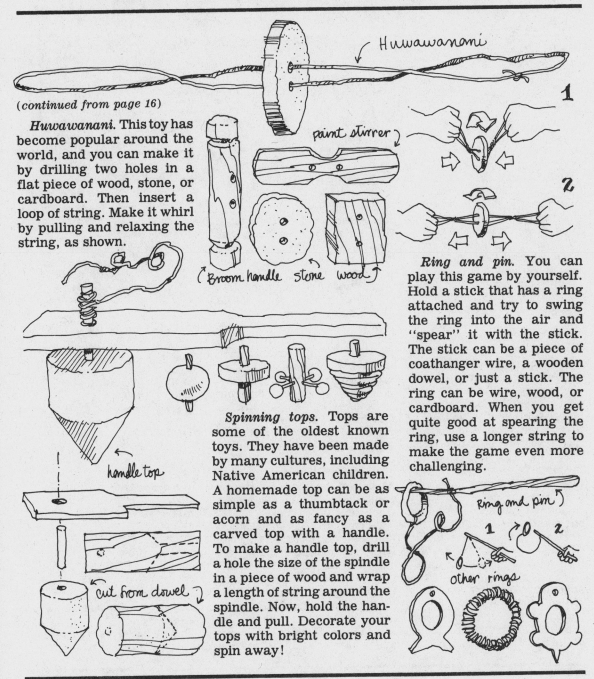

(*continued from page 16*)

Huwawanani. This toy has become popular around the world, and you can make it by drilling two holes in a flat piece of wood, stone, or cardboard. Then insert a loop of string. Make it whirl by pulling and relaxing the string, as shown.

Huwawanani

paint stirrer

Broom handle   stone   wood

1

2

handle top

cut from dowel

Spinning tops. Tops are some of the oldest known toys. They have been made by many cultures, including Native American children. A homemade top can be as simple as a thumbtack or acorn and as fancy as a carved top with a handle. To make a handle top, drill a hole the size of the spindle in a piece of wood and wrap a length of string around the spindle. Now, hold the handle and pull. Decorate your tops with bright colors and spin away!

Ring and pin. You can play this game by yourself. Hold a stick that has a ring attached and try to swing the ring into the air and "spear" it with the stick. The stick can be a piece of coathanger wire, a wooden dowel, or just a stick. The ring can be wire, wood, or cardboard. When you get quite good at spearing the ring, use a longer string to make the game even more challenging.

ring and pin

1   2

other rings

The Animal Zoetrope
or Making the Elephant Run

THE STRIP OF "FILM" IS DROPPED INSIDE THE CARTON AND RESTS ON THE BOTTOM.

1 INCH APART

1 INCH DOWN

EACH SLOT IS 4 INCHES LONG AND 1/8 INCH WIDE.

← DRAW FROM RIGHT TO LEFT. ←

END

START

THE OUTSIDE OF THE CARTON IS PAINTED BLACK.

Did you try the "Elephant Pie" on page 55? If you did, you may already know the secret of making the elephant run. But even if you know the secret, you should make a zoetrope. Because your baby sister will love it. So will you. (You like movies, don't you?)

First the Zoetrope

To make the zoetrope, *you'll need:* a big cardboard ice cream box (the round kind that you see in ice cream stores), a single-edge razor blade, or sharp paper knife, and some black paint. You'll also need to borrow the family phonograph turntable, but not until later.

The hardest part is cutting the slots. Make a circle of vertical slots all around the carton. Measure carefully. They should be an inch apart and one-eighth inch wide. If the slots are uneven, your movie will be jerky. Be very careful with the razor blade or knife. Get someone to help you if you have trouble. After the slots are cut, find the center of the bottom of the carton and cut an X there. Now paint the *outside* of the carton with black paint.

Then the Movies

You might start with the elephant, but it doesn't matter. With your zoetrope and some drawings you can make *anything* run! To make a film, cut a strip of paper that is four inches wide and long enough to fit inside the carton without overlapping at the ends. Now tape the paper strip to the inside of the carton at the top and make a light pencil mark through each slot. Take the strip off and lay it out flat. The idea is to make one drawing between each pencil mark. If you have 15 pencil marks, it means your action must take 14 drawings, each one changing in equal amounts. Make good, simple, strong drawings using a dark line. Felt-tipped pens are good. You can add color later if you like.

When the film is done, put it inside the carton *at the bottom,* with the drawings facing *inside.* Put the X on the carton bottom down on the spindle of the phonograph turntable, look through the slots, and shine a light into it. Then turn on the turntable at the slowest speed and watch the action! *Other*

SHINE A LIGHT INSIDE THE CARTON.

TURN THE PHONOGRAPH TO ITS LOWEST SPEED.

Movies: Baby Sister Has a Tantrum. Dodo the Dancing Dog. The Cat and the Mouse. Moon over Miami. Eating a Hamburger. Or you think of some.

P.S. What does "zoetrope" mean, anyway?

Male oryx antelopes have long and very sharp horns, which can be weapons; the antelopes can stab an attacking lion with them. When two male antelopes fight each other, they never use their horns. They fight by pushing their heads against each other, and if the horns happen to touch each other's body, they stop, then start the fight over.

Birds have special muscles in their skin for fluffing out their feathers. You have similar muscles; they're the ones that give you "goose bumps." Birds that look fat on cold days are using these muscles.

Mistletoe is a twiggy plant that lives high up in trees as a parasite on branches. Mistletoe has an interesting word history. In the Anglo-Saxon language, *mistel tan* means "the little dung twig." Long ago people noticed that birds ate mistletoe berries and that new plants grew where birds excreted the berries. In fact, they believed that mistletoe would not sprout unless the berry had ripened in a bird's stomach.

Some insects that live in caves have, during the ages, lost their eyes completely. Still, many of these will scurry out of the beam of a light shined on them. Apparently, they can sense light with their skins.

The largest of Saturn's moons, Titan, is larger than the planet Mercury.

Scientists are investigating the possibility of towing icebergs to dry, populated places such as Los Angeles and Saudi Arabia. Antarctic icebergs are as big as 150 miles across and 1,000 feet thick. Tugboats would take eight to ten months to push and pull one from Antarctica's McMurdo Sound to Los Angeles. It's a wild idea, but people in many places around the world need much more water than they have.

Monday November 28

Tuesday November 29

Wednesday November 30

Thursday December 1
First Night of Jewish Festival of Lights, Hanukah

Friday December 2

Saturday December 3

Sunday December 4
Annular Solar Eclipse
7:20 A.M.

New Moon
●

Monday December 5
Tuesday December 6
Wednesday December 7
Thursday December 8
Friday December 9
Saturday December 10 *Make Footprint Papers for your holiday gifts. See page 79.*
Sunday December 11

Because it is always green and has no roots in the ground, mistletoe has been surrounded with mystery and superstition for centuries. People who lived in places with long harsh winters thought of it as a sign of everlasting life and likened it to the human soul. American mistletoe is the state flower of Oklahoma. During their first hard winters there, it was the only green plant the early pioneers could find to put on the graves of their dead.

Chameleons are small lizards that can change colors. To defend itself, the chameleon will match its color to the color of the surface it's on, so it can't be seen easily. At other times it wants to be noticed and can change to an attracting color. Many lizards can do this, but chameleons are the best at it.

A black hole is the opposite of a star. A star shines, giving off heat and light. A black hole pulls everything into itself, even light. A black hole is invisible because light cannot "escape" to show us where it is.

The red color of the poinsettia is carried by its leaves. The flowers of this plant are in the center of the ring of leaves and are very small.

Living in the wild, animals rarely live out the number of years they can in captivity. Here are the greatest ages reached by animals kept in zoos and laboratories: baboon, 35; polar bear, 34; camel, 29; chipmunk, 8; Asian elephant, 70; giraffe, 33; guinea pig, 7; lion, 25; sea lion, 28; tiger, 26.

The green spots on rotten oranges are penicillin mold, the same source from which we get the miracle drug penicillin. The silvery dust on grapes and plums is really a coat of wild yeasts.

The Holidays Are Coming

Are You Ready?

About this story. Several years ago Harriett Weaver read a newspaper account about a young boy who lost his dog and found him again under very unusual circumstances. You'll see how unusual they were when you read this Christmas story. Although the writer has made certain changes, her story is based upon events that really happened.

Tony's Christmas Eve

by Harriett E. Weaver

A heavy snow was falling. The night would have been coal black except for the snow crystals, glistening and sparkling in the glow of the street lamps. Underfoot, ice crunched as workers plodded wearily homeward. For many days the thermometer had hovered near zero. Christmas was not far away.

Within the friendly light of a downtown store window stood a newsboy. He shifted from one foot to the other, stamping hard each time, trying to warm himself. Under one arm were several copies of the evening edition still to be sold. In the crook of the other arm he snuggled a small brown dog, quite young like his master. At this moment the pup was gazing out at the world so quickly whitened. Every now and

then he tucked his nose more deeply into the woolly scarf that had been wrapped around him tightly. It was scarcely enough for real warmth; yet he would rather shiver out there with Tony than be comfortable and cozy anywhere else. Twice already this winter he had escaped through an opened door at home and scampered down the street, just to be with his master—one time in a near blizzard.

"Paper, sir?" he called hopefully to a man who was hurrying by. The man forced onward as if he had not heard. As if to make up for the disappointment, the boy hugged his little dog more tightly and pressed his cheek gently against the shaggy face. Two very dark eyes opened and looked up through the strands of brown hair drooping down from the top of his head. In them gleamed the sparkle of a love that filled him, warming him much more than the woolly scarf.

"It won't be long now, Muffy," Tony told him. Soon afterwards the last paper was sold. With all the papers gone at last and his work over for the day, the boy ducked into a hotel lobby and sought the steam heat of its radiator. There Tony dried and warmed the woolly scarf. Then he rewrapped his pet, leaving only a small hole for breathing.

"We will be home soon, Muffy," he assured the dog.

Down the street at a violin maker's shop, the lad gazed through the frosted window for a moment before he entered. A bell attached to the door tinkled his arrival. Behind the counter an old Italian man bent over a workbench. Upon hearing the bell, he laid aside his glasses and looked up expectantly.

Antonio Corelli was stooped and frail, but he brightened when he saw his grandson. A radiant love lighted his eyes as he drew the boy into the welcome of his arms. Tony smiled contentedly. Home at last!

The dog huddled close to the woodstove. Almost at once the heat cast its spell. Muffy glanced around, bleary-eyed; then he relaxed and nearly toppled over as he fell asleep.

"Your supper is in the back room, Tony," the old man said. "Let us eat. I know you are hungry and cold."

"And you, Nonno?" Tony asked, peering into his grandfather's face. "What about the violin?"

The old violin maker beamed happily. "It is finished."

He took it from the workbench and handed it to his grandson. His eyes shone as he watched the boy caress the instrument, fingering its strings as though it were almost too precious to touch.

"It's perfect," the boy murmured admiringly.

"A Corelli made it," the old man reminded him proudly.

Antonio Corelli was not a man who was feeble in old age. But the work and a long life of poverty had begun to tell. Too many times there had not been enough to eat.

Tony and his nonno were alone now—the last of their family. Tony felt keenly a sense of his own responsibility, so how could he look upon braving the cold of a drafty street corner after school as a real hardship? To him it seemed like a privilege. He liked knowing that he was man enough at ten to take his place among those who worked and earned.

This lifestyle of necessity rather than of pleasure had been too difficult for Tony to have become much of a dreamer. In daily living hard facts had to be faced. Each one required careful planning and, too often, just raw endurance. Yet he did dream. Always in his heart there was a desire to change things for the better.

Nutkins
Lots of Fun in a Nutshell

This is how to make a nutshell into a racing car or a frightened mouse or a fast beetle or anything else that scoots. *You'll need:* some small marbles, some big walnuts, some glue, paint, and bits of stuff for eyes, ears, and so forth.

Pick out the biggest walnuts and carefully crack them in half. You need the entire half-shell for each nutkin. Scrape out the meat and hard membrane inside. Decorate the outside of each shell (that's important).

The nutkin scoots because of the marble under each shell. When the nutkin is placed on a sloping surface, it runs downhill. So you'll also need to make a ramp. Any smooth, tilted surface will do. Can you make the nutkin run uphill? Whose nutkin scoots fastest? If a nutkin is made from a walnut shell, what is a cupkin? A cankin?

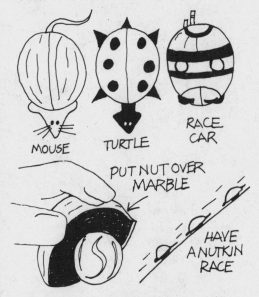

P.S. A nest of nutkins might make a fine present for your brother or sister who has everything.

A Winter Wreath

If you've started a collection of dried leaves, seedpods, and other plant parts, now is a good time to put them to use by making a wonderful winter wreath. There is no end to the combination of things that can be put together, and there is no end to the way they can be put together, either. Get your dried plant parts together and draw up a plan. In addition, *you'll need:* a piece of plywood or masonite about 18 inches square, white glue, a drill, and a roll of florist's or other fine wire.

Lay the parts you want to use on a piece of paper. Arrange them in a circle about the same size as the wood backing. It's very disappointing to get part way around the circle and run out of material, so make the circle smaller if you need to. Then ask an adult to help you cut the wood into a doughnut shape the same size as your circle. After the wood is cut, drill many holes all over it. Bulky parts may be attached to the back by "sewing" them with the wire or thread through these holes.

Work from large pieces to small ones and from flat to lumpy for the best results. Flat, glossy leaves laid overlapping can be sewn to the base (or glued) and are an especially pretty covering. Saw pine cones into slices, like bread. They make nice, flat flower disks. Arrange these with seedpods and other smaller parts.

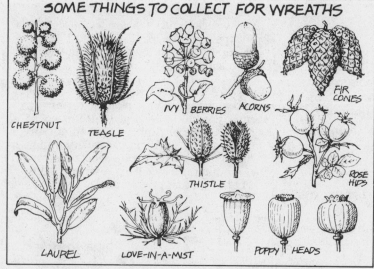

SOME THINGS TO COLLECT FOR WREATHS

CHESTNUT

TEASLE

IVY BERRIES

ACORNS

FIR CONES

THISTLE

ROSE HIPS

LAUREL

LOVE-IN-A-MIST

POPPY HEADS

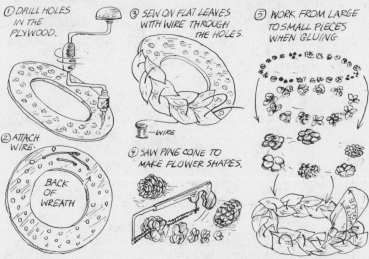

① DRILL HOLES IN THE PLYWOOD.

② ATTACH WIRE.

BACK OF WREATH

③ SEW ON FLAT LEAVES WITH WIRE THROUGH THE HOLES.

—WIRE

④ SAW PINE CONE TO MAKE FLOWER SHAPES.

⑤ WORK FROM LARGE TO SMALL PIECES WHEN GLUING

The nicest wreaths have many parts and are thick and bushy. Because they are made of dried things they will last a long time. They are fun to make, and people love to receive them as gifts.

This evening, in the living quarters back of the shop, Tony and his grandfather ate their meager supper and fed Muffin the scraps. There was little to delight, much less satisfy, the demands of a growing boy's appetite, but presently the warmth of the minestrone soup set his blood to tingling. And there were a few crackers to go with it.

Muffin got most of the crackers, with some of the minestrone poured over them. They had nothing else for him just then. Feeling disturbed about this, Tony took the shaggy little head in his hands and tipped the face up so he might better look into the brown eyes. In them sparkled a love that lack of a good meal could never dull. When he saw this, a glint of determination replaced the usual glow in his own eyes. His heart raced.

"I'm going to do something about this, Muffy," he vowed through tight lips. "I want for you the things that make you strong. Everything you like. Bowls full, too, not just bits left over. I wish us all to have good things, like other people. I want for Nonno . . ."

Muffin was listening no longer. He had gone to the other side of the room and was leaning against the violin case standing in the corner, the one with Tony's name on it.

"Ho! I bet you want me to play *Ave Maria*," Tony exclaimed, forgetting his dark thoughts. Then with a merry laugh, "You know what is beautiful and pleasing to the ear."

Muffin must have because he watched the opening of the violin case with as much interest as if he expected a string of sausages to jump out.

Meanwhile, Antonio Corelli had gone back into the shop and was fondling the instrument he had completed that day, now placing it carefully in its new velvet-lined case, now running his fingers over the satinlike finish.

Just then the bell on the shop door tinkled, and he looked up to see a tall, well-dressed man enter.

"Good evening, Mr. Corelli. I thought I'd drop in to ask if perhaps my violin is ready. Ah! Do I see it there?" With a nod of his head he indicated the instrument lying in its case on the workbench.

"You do, indeed, Mr. DiBernardi," was the reply. "It is my finest. The tone is soft and mellow. You will see. Try it."

Rafael DiBernardi placed the violin carefully under his chin. His anticipation showed in every move as he prepared to draw the bow across the strings. Before the bow touched the strings, however, there came from the back room the soft tones of another violin. First a slow dreamy prelude that seemed to drift on the air; then in throaty strength, the first strains of Schubert's *Ave Maria*—each note clear and distinct, the main theme smooth and exact. Listening intently, Mr.

DiBernardi lowered his own instrument. His eyes widened as he stared toward the closed door of the Corelli living quarters while the music went on.

"Who, may I ask, can play like *that!*" he asked.

"That is my grandson, Tony. He is a Corelli."

"Grandson? He must be a genius. May I see him?"

After the final strains of the *Ave Maria* had died away, the young violinist was summoned. The door opened, and he came forward, violin in hand, Muffin at his heels.

"Tony, my boy, come meet Mr. DiBernardi. He is the violinist we hear over KQX. He is a soloist with the city symphony.

The visitor's face reflected his amazement. "You mean it was *you* playing the *Ave Maria* . . . like that? I thought surely you were much older."

Tony smiled shyly and reached down to pet a brown, furry body that had bunched up against his legs. "I play for Muffy," he said. "He likes *Ave Maria*. It is his favorite."

"I imagine so," Mr. DiBernardi replied with feeling. "It is one of mine too."

Tony shifted from one foot to the other, reaching down to scratch Muffy's ears fondly. For a moment or two there was silence in the shop. Mr. DiBernardi appeared to be mulling something over in his mind. All at once he took a deep breath and said, "My boy, how would you like to make hundreds, yes, thousands, happy with your violin?"

Wonder flooded Tony's face. "Why, how much I would like to, sir, but how? I'm afraid I don't see . . ."

The Footprint Papers

Who's been walking on the gift wrap?

RABBIT

FOX

RACCOON

MOUSE

BLACK BEAR

BADGER

DEER

Try your hand at making animal-track wrapping paper. If animals aren't doing much walking (and leaving prints) in your neighborhood, here are a few prints we've found for you. Choose your favorites and get started. *You'll need:* some large sheets of newsprint, or other plain paper, and something to carve your tracks in—either potatoes or small linoleum blocks will work. You'll also need a small knife or linoleum cutters and some poster paint or block-printing ink.

First copy the designs onto paper. Make your drawing the size you want to print. Keep it as simple as you can. Avoid small intricate shapes. Then copy the design onto the block. If you are using a potato, use the point of your knife to scratch the design outline. If you are making linoleum blocks, draw it with a pencil.

The next step is to cut away everything that isn't animal track. *Be careful.* Cutting tools can hurt you. Always cut *away* from your body or hands. Go slowly.

Use thick poster paint or block-printing ink to print with. Apply a smooth and even coat of paint or ink to your block. Use a brush or small roller. The rest is up to your imagination. You can combine various colors, and different animals, in any kind of regular or random pattern.

When you wrap a gift in this kind of paper, see if the person who opens it can guess which animals walked there! (P.S. What kind of track does *your* totem animal make?)

PUT LAYERS OF NEWSPAPER UNDERNEATH.

Cut the tracks of your totem animal in a block, then use the block to leave your special mark on letters, signs, and other personal items.

STATIONERY

BOXES

BOOK COVERS

Tin Can Lanterns

Here is a good way to recycle a few tin cans *and* make a fine present for your mom, or some other grownup. *You'll need:* some tin cans, an assortment of nails (different sizes make different size holes), a hammer, some paper and tape, and the use of a freezer for a day and a night. You'll also need one short candle for each can. Cut the paper to fit around the outside of each can. Then fill the cans with water and leave them in the freezer until it freezes. A day and night, at least.

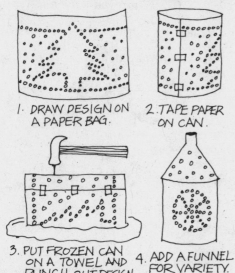

1. DRAW DESIGN ON A PAPER BAG.

2. TAPE PAPER ON CAN.

3. PUT FROZEN CAN ON A TOWEL AND PUNCH OUT DESIGN.

4. ADD A FUNNEL FOR VARIETY.

While the water is freezing, make your designs on the paper. Put a dot where you want each hole. When the water is frozen, tape the paper pattern on each can, laying it on a towel while you work. The ice inside makes it easy to punch a hole, using the nail and hammer, without denting the can. Empty the cans and dry them, then you are ready to light them.

Mr. DiBernardi by now was full of his idea. He smiled.

"On Christmas Eve the KQX television station is sponsoring holiday entertainment at the Eastside Auditorium. Several motion picture stars have volunteered their talents. We're going to have a Christmas play, and a well-known choir will sing carols. If you would play the *Ave Maria,* as you did a few moments ago, what a perfect closing for a beautiful evening that would be! Will you?" Mr. DiBernardi asked.

Tony's eyes lighted up as he listened to this invitation. He didn't know what to say. It was all so unexpected, so overwhelming. In desperation he cast an inquiring glance at his grandfather. When a gentle smile told him that there was no question about approval, he brightened even more. Scarcely able to contain himself, Tony struggled to find words. Then in a rush of delight and anticipation they came tumbling out. "Yes, sir, of course I'll play. I'll play my whole heart," he cried eagerly.

The days that followed flew by. Once the evening papers were sold, Tony headed for the shop—on the run. Every possible minute he worked at perfecting the *Ave Maria* for Christmas Eve. He lost interest in mingling with the crowds that clustered around the holiday window displays down the street. Far more important and exciting things filled his thoughts. Wasn't he to be the only one of the city's Italian community to appear on a Christmas television program that was going to be viewed all over the country?

The thrill of it all blotted out the disappointment of knowing that for the two Corellis there would be no Christmas filled with all the pretty decorations and delicious holiday goodies and surprises, gaily wrapped and ribboned.

Long ago the work to help his grandfather provide even the essentials had replaced the carefree fun of other boys and girls his age. There never was money left over for little extras. But Tony had his violin, old, cherished, and mellowed. A real treasure, handed down through several generations of Corellis. A priceless treasure. Into it he poured his happiness, his sadness, his world. Always there to listen and understand was his nonno and, of course, Muffin, his constant pal of both home and street corner—his delight.

It was two weeks before Christmas. Bareheaded, his coat missing, Tony sped wildly down the street, zigzagging across crowded intersections, plunging through the holiday jam of a shopping center. Stark despair and terror convulsed his face. He ran into the violin shop, flung himself down, breathless and exhausted, at his grandfather's side. No little brown shag dog romped in with him.

"Nonno! It's Muffy. He's gone! The big newsboy that has been trying to take over my corner pushed me down, grabbed Muffy, and ran. He said he's . . . he's going to drown him in the river. I could not catch him."

His panic and grief were shattering. Beloved Muffy was gone, and Muffy was life itself. In a flood the tears came. The loss seemed too much for him to bear.

At that moment the heart went out of Tony. Nothing his nonno could say or do eased his grief in the least. The violin playing continued day after day, but woodenly, without feeling.

Christmas drew ever nearer, and Tony went about his work, pale and silent. Gently, whenever he could, the old violin maker held him close and talked to him, trying desperately to comfort. But it was no use. Nothing he could say or do eased the torment that tore at his grandson.

Christmas Eve finally came. Tony donned his best, such as it was. After placing his violin in its case with tender care, he waited for Rafael DiBernardi, who was to call for him and his grandfather. Tense, pale, and hollow eyed, he sat stiffly on a chair. The joy that had been Tony's was now far, far away.

Antonio Corelli placed a hand on his grandson's shoulder and said quietly, "My son, you are the chosen one tonight. In a little while you will present your greatest gift. Tony glanced up and tried to smile, but tears filled his eyes. "I loved Muffy so, Nonno. I have no heart for playing. I have no heart for it anymore. Something is gone."

The elder Corelli thought for a minute, then spoke in a low voice, "Wherever Muffy is, he will hear you. He will be with you. He will sit by you when you play the *Ave Maria* as he always did. Tony, listen to me. *The beloved never die.*"

Peaceable Kingdom Cookies

We all know that most creatures are dinner to some other creatures. That is how nature operates. But there are stories about how all the animals used to live together in a kingdom that was full of peace and harmony. Who can be sure it wasn't that way once long ago?

You can make your own peaceable kingdom and use the animals to decorate a Christmas tree, or anything else for the holiday season. You could cut them from cardboard and paint them. But the nicest way is to make them from cookie dough. Choose some animals from the drawings on this page, then copy the animals the size you want. About four inches across is probably best. In addition to the ingredients listed in the recipe below, *you'll need:* a small paring knife for cutting the shapes in the rolled-out dough, some short macaroni, and colored paper or cloth ribbons for hangers.

1 Set oven at 375°.

2 Heat to the boiling point:
- ½ cup molasses

3 Add:
- ¼ cup sugar
- 3 tablespoons butter or other shortening
- 1 tablespoon milk

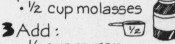

4 Sift together:
- 2 cups flour
- ½ teaspoon *each* of baking soda, salt, nutmeg,

cinnamon, powdered cloves, and ginger.

5 Add to the first mixture. *Add more flour if necessary to make dough thick enough to roll out.*

6 Shape mixture into a ball. Roll out on a floured board to ¼ inch thick.

Before you bake the cookies, decide where you want the hole for hanging them. Using a piece of the macaroni, punch a hole in the dough and remove the dough plug from the macaroni. Put the macaroni back into the hole to keep it open

7 Cut into animal shapes. Remember to poke a hole with a piece of macaroni so your animal can be laced with a ribbon and tied to your tree.

8 Arrange cookies on a buttered cookie sheet or a cookie sheet that has been lined with aluminum foil.

9 Bake 8 to 10 minutes.

while it bakes. After the cookies have cooled, thread colored ribbon through each hole and tie a loop for hanging.

Now, if this is a peaceable kingdom, *you'll* have to decide whether or not to eat these animal cookies.

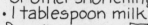

The big auditorium was jammed to its second balcony with hundreds of happy, excited people. It was a happy time. The gaily decorated Christmas tree onstage, the ribboned wreaths at every window, the fragrance of pine and fir brought sparkle to the eyes of everyone.

At last the auditorium was darkened, and the big curtains parted. For over an hour the city's best talent held the crowd spellbound. First, a big church choir sang Christmas carols, then a college group presented a holiday play. After that a movie star told a Christmas story, a Spanish guitar group played holiday songs of old Mexico, and the recreation center's Black glee club sang spirituals. From the first moment, when Rafael DiBernardi stepped onstage to act as master of ceremonies, television lights and cameras zeroed in on the action.

Now Mr. DiBernardi was onstage again, adjusting the microphone and waiting for quiet. "Dear Christmas guests," he began in that resonant voice of his, "it is my pleasure to introduce a brand new star. Tonight is to be his first public appearance, but believe me, it will not be his last. This richly talented lad may be young in years; but already, as you will see and hear, he shows unusual promise. In the future we will come to know him well, for his destiny is that of greatness. I'm proud to be the one to present him, a young man of just ten, who represents the wonderful Italian people of our fine city, and who also . . ."

Offstage, Tony turned breathlessly to the old man standing close beside him. "Nonno, I can't play. I . . . I just can't, can't even remember the notes or . . ."

"Yes, you can," the old one put in quietly, his voice steady and calm. "You are well prepared. You have worked hard. You can be very sure of yourself." Gentle concern seemed to deepen the lines of the grandfather's kindly face as he held the violin out to his grandson.

Tony hesitated. For a moment he looked as if he wondered what he was doing there. Then he shook his head and glanced wildly around backstage, actually seeing none of it. "I can't, Nonno," he kept repeating. And then finally, "If Muffy were just here with me . . . but now I can't. I don't know what happened to him."

"Muffy is here, my boy," the old man said softly. "I know he is somehow waiting for you out there. Play for him. He will surely hear you, for music is all language and crosses all boundaries. Now go make the *Ave Maria* a benediction to a beautiful sacred evening, your greeting from all of us to the holy day that comes tomorrow."

Tony, listening to his grandfather, calmed.

Once Rafael DiBernardi's introduction was completed, the crowd broke into applause. Hearing it, Tony nodded, sighed deeply, and straightened. Then slowly, as if to himself, he murmured, "I'll play my best. For Nonno, for Muffy." Then he added, "But I don't think I'll ever play again."

Tony walked onstage and took his place beside the piano, where his accompanist sat. Lost in his own thoughts, he was unaware of the stir that his appearance had caused in the packed auditorium.

With the first notes of the piano introduction Tony tucked the violin under his chin. At the right moment he raised the bow.

In tones that were scarcely audible came the opening strains of the *Ave Maria*. Sad and throaty they were, but true and beautiful and majestic. Swelling on and on, they told only too well of the anguish that tore at a boy bereft of his dog. Tony's thoughts were for Muffy. Muffy who would never be there anymore to lean against his legs as though he couldn't get close enough to the music.

On wings of sound the *Ave Maria* mounted ever higher until in a plaintive harmony of strings it swept to the very rafters of the packed auditorium. There it seemed to hover. Hushed and awed, the audience sat forward in their seats, feeling response deep within themselves.

Then, slowly, those alongside one aisle became aware of a soft pit-pat-pit-pat. A few heads turned, in annoyance at first, and then in wonder.

Midway in the aisle, his coat still glistening with snowflakes, sat a small, brown shag dog. He was so pitifully thin that his ribs showed plainly, but in his black eyes burned a fire. One cold forepaw half-raised, he appeared unsure of himself. He glanced nervously around at those staring down at him.

The earth floor beneath a grove of eucalyptus trees is bare. The fragrant leaves of these trees make a toxin, a substance that other plants cannot bear. When the leaves fall, rain carries the toxin into the soil and keeps other plants from growing there.

It's marvelous to think that the crystals of no two snowflakes are alike, but some scientists think that may not be true. Even they would admit, though, that the chances of two being the same shape are very small.

Bloodhounds are the champion sniffers among all dogs. Police use them to help hunt for kids who have gotten lost. The bloodhound's face looks sad, but the sad parts of it actually help it with its smelling. Its droopy ears stir up scents from the ground, and the wrinkles in its face form pockets where scents are trapped.

*The chill is on from
near and far
In all the months that
have an R.*

Sable and marten grow lots of fine hair beneath their longer bristles as winter begins. This double coat traps air and so increases insulation and helps the animal hold onto the heat its body produces. The soles of the feet of Arctic foxes become furry in winter. This not only keeps the paws warm, but also helps the whole foot to work like a snowshoe.

A species of wild parakeet once lived in North America as far north as New York. For a time it was the fashion to wear hats that had stuffed parakeets attached to them. Now this species is extinct; the last one was seen in Florida in 1904. Today wild parakeets are found in Australia, Africa, and Asia.

First Quarter Moon ◑

Monday December 12

Tuesday December 13

Wednesday December 14

Thursday December 15

Friday December 16

Saturday December 17

Sunday December 18

Monday December 19	Penumbral Lunar Eclipse 8:49 P.M. Full Moon ○
Tuesday December 20	
Wednesday December 21	
Thursday December 22	Winter Solstice
Friday December 23	
Saturday December 24	
Sunday December 25 *Christmas Day*	

The aardvark is the champion digger of the animal kingdom. With its powerful claws it can burrow out of sight in soft soil far more quickly than a man using a shovel. Its ears can turn around, so dirt doesn't enter them while the aardvark is digging. This animal has excellent hearing—it can hear ants on the march. Its long sticky tongue gathers up the ants.

A snow crystal needs a nucleus to start growing. This may be dust from a field, ash from a volcanic eruption, exhaust gas from city traffic, salt spray from the ocean, or even a tiny living thing (micro-organism). What form the crystal will take depends largely on temperature and how much water vapor is in the air.

Guinea pigs are not pigs. They are rodents, the family that includes mice, squirrels, and beavers. The Incas of South America were keeping them as pets at the time Spanish explorers arrived in the New World. Dutch traders took guinea pigs to Europe. Today they are commonly used in laboratory experiments to test medicines.

Some unusual plants can capture and devour animals, but there are no *human*-eating plants. The largest creatures these carnivorous plants can capture are small frogs. The animal touches a "trigger" on the plant, and leaves or other plant parts quickly close around it. Juices made by the plant digest the meal.

After its old skin splits, a growing insect simply crawls out of it. Its new skin is very soft and delicate. The insect may then swallow a lot of air or water to expand its size as much as possible while the new skin hardens. The hardening happens within a few minutes.

They watched the little fellow totter toward the stage. Several times he stopped for a moment, weary and drooping. At the foot of the stage steps he hesitated again, this time to gaze longingly up at the young violinist.

Tony was playing as if in a dream, playing his heart out. Eyes closed, he could see his Muffy there beside him, just as he had always been.

Summoning what strength was left, the little dog dragged himself up the steps and on to centerstage. There, out of both weakness and pure joy—and because he was *home*—he relaxed contentedly against Tony's leg.

The boy's eyes flew open. A flood of color rushed into his face. He knew now that somehow Muffy had heard. The dog nestled closer. Amazed and fascinated, the big audience watched Tony's lips part in a beaming smile.

The music seemed to come alive as it surged into the finale of the *Ave Maria*. When at last it had faded away, Tony dropped to his knees and hugged the furry body to his heart. Through tears he peered once more into the shining eyes of his pal.

And Muffy? He tucked a cold nose under the chin where the violin had rested and sighed a big sigh.

Answers

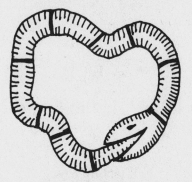

Hoop Snake, page 5

There are 24 birds hidden in the illustration on page 8. How many did you find?

Chicken Fences, page 10

Sleeping-Alligator Sneak, page 23

Monday December 26	Last Quarter Moon ◑
Tuesday December 27	
Wednesday December 28	
Thursday December 29	
Friday December 30	
Saturday December 31 *New Year's Eve*	

Do you have your 1984 Kids for Nature Yearbook yet?

The kiwi is a bird that can't fly. It lays an egg that weighs more than one pound, which is about one-fourth of the kiwi's weight. The bird's nostrils are at the end of its long bill, not at the base of it. When the kiwi pokes its bill into the soil, its excellent sense of smell can find what its very small eyes cannot.

The major flow of air over the United States is from west to east. If this were the only movement of air above us, we could be quite sure about the approaching weather. But this flow runs into cold air from the north and has to climb over high mountain ranges, making our weather much more unpredictable and complicated.

*Mackerel scales and mares' tails
Make lofty ships carry low sails.*

Over the ages, some fish species that live in totally dark caves have become blind; eyes are of no use to them. Even though they do not have external ears, fish can hear. Sound vibrations pass much more easily through water than through air. Not only does a fish live in water, but its body is mostly water too. Inner ears pick up vibrations from water and transmit messages to the brain.

*Yellow streaks in sunset sky
Wind and daylong rain is nigh.*

The oldest living trees on earth are thought to be bristlecone pines in California's White Mountains. Some are an estimated 4,600 years old. The oldest redwood trees are about 3,500 years old.

Scientists think that all the continents on earth were once joined together in one giant continent they call "Pangaea." The theory is that the seven continents moved to their present positions by drifting on vast "plates" of solid rock. The bumping of the plates can explain why there are earthquakes and how mountains were formed.

ANNOUNCING
THE FIRST SIERRA CLUB
KIDS FOR NATURE CONTESTS

Draw a picture, take a photograph, write a story, and
win terrific prizes!

See rules and entry blanks on the following pages

There are three contests, with a first, second, and third
prizewinner in each contest. Enter any one or all three. All
contest winners will have their artwork, photographs, and
stories published in the *1984 Kids for Nature Yearbook*. But
don't delay. The deadline for entries is February 20, 1983.

First prize

First prize in each contest will be a one-week Sierra Club Family Outing for you and your parents or guardians. The prize includes all travel expenses, including air fare. The Sierra Club has been taking people into the great wildernesses of America since the beginning of this century. Trips for prizewinners will take place in August of 1983. Family Outings take place in many parts of the country, including the Sierra Nevada, the Idaho Rockies, the Southwest, and in eastern woodlands and waterways. All trips are led by experienced people.*

Second prize

Second prize in each contest is a $300 gift certificate from Eastern Mountain Sports (EMS) or Recreational Equipment, Inc. (REI Coop), two of the largest retailers of outdoor equipment in the country. Pick out your choice of clothing, sleeping bags, backpacks, tents, cross-country skis, and much more. Make your choice from the catalog, or visit the nearest REI or EMS store.

Third prize

Third prize in each contest is a $100 gift certificate from EMS or REI Coop.

---

*Sierra Club will select the outings to be awarded to prizewinners. Details and locations of 1983 trips are not available at time of publication. Winners will be notified of trip details when winners are announced in April 1983. Prize includes all costs for winner and two additional family members, one of whom must be a parent or guardian. Other family members may be included subject to available space, at the family's expense. All participants in Sierra Club Family Outings are subject to screening by outing leaders.

How to Enter
CONTEST 1
FOR THE BEST DRAWINGS
OR PAINTINGS

The winners of this contest will be the persons who have submitted the best original drawings or paintings of any subject from nature. You may draw animals, plants, people, and any other natural subjects.

Only original freehand work can be accepted. You may submit as many as three pieces of artwork. Attach a separate entry form (or copy) to each entry. Drawings or paintings may be done in any medium, including pencil, pen and ink, charcoal, pastels, watercolor, oil, tempera, and acrylic.

If your artwork is not done on stiff drawing board, it should be protected by heavy cardboard when it is wrapped for mailing. Please do not send artwork that is framed or packages that include any glass.

How to Enter
CONTEST 2
FOR THE BEST
PHOTOGRAPHS

The winners of this contest will be the persons who have submitted the best photographs of a natural subject. The photographs may be either color or black and white. They may show any subject from nature: scenics, plants, wildlife, or people in natural settings.

Entries may be submitted as color transparencies, color prints, or black-and-white prints. *Please do not submit negatives.* Prints may be any size. You may submit as many as three photographs. Attach a separate entry form (or copy) to each entry. All entries should be protected by heavy cardboard when they are wrapped for mailing. Please do not send photographs that are framed or packages that contain any glass.

How to Enter
CONTEST 3
FOR THE BEST
SHORT STORIES

The winners of this contest will be the persons who have submitted the best short stories about the world of nature and the great outdoors. Your story may be nonfiction—that is a true tale about something that actually happened. Or it may be fiction—that is a story made up from your imagination. Anything you submit must be original—told in your own words.

Your story should be at least 300 words long (about one typed page) but not more than 1,000 words long (about three to four typed pages). Please use plain white paper. Type your story if you can. Or you may write it clearly, using ink. Be sure you give your story a title.

You may submit as many as three stories. Attach a separate entry form (or copy) to each entry.

Be sure to read the contest rules on the next page.

91

Be sure to read these
CONTEST RULES

1. To enter any of the contests you must be 12 years old or *younger*.

2. You can enter one, two, or all three of the contests if you want to. There is no charge for entering the contests, and no purchase is required.

3. With each separate entry you send in you must include an entry blank from this Yearbook (see pages 93 and 95), or a clearly written or typed copy of the entry blank containing the same information.

4. All entries must be postmarked no later than February 20, 1983. Address your entries to Kids for Nature Contests, Sierra Club Books, 530 Bush Street, San Francisco, CA 94108.

5. We will return all original artwork and photographs, but we cannot return stories—please keep a copy.

6. Contest winners will be notified by mail not before April 1, 1983, and not later than May 1, 1983. Results of the contest will also be announced in the *1984 Kids for Nature Yearbook.*

7. Entries will be judged by a panel composed of Sierra Club staff and professional writers, artists, and photographers. The decisions of the judges will be final. Entries will be judged on the basis of content, skill in execution, relevance to environmental themes, and overall artistic effect, all as evaluated by the judges.

8. Entries will be accepted only from addresses within those of the fifty United States that do not prohibit, restrict, license, or tax the contests. No employee of the Sierra Club, Charles Scribner's Sons, The Yolla Bolly Press, J. Walter Thompson, or any affiliated organization, or any member of the immediate family of any such employee may enter the contests. All members of the Sierra Club are eligible unless excluded by the previous sentence.

9. All publication rights and copyrights associated with the winning entries become the exclusive property of Sierra Club Books. Sierra Club Books may use the winning entries and exercise those rights (or refrain from doing either) in any manner Sierra Club Books considers appropriate. Sierra Club Books will have no obligation to any winning contestant beyond that of providing that contestant with the prize awarded.

10. Payment of any income, sales, or other taxes on a prize is the responsibility of the winner of the prize. Taxes, if any, will not be paid by Sierra Club Books.

11. Sierra Club Books is in no manner responsible or liable for any warranty, representation, or guarantee, express or implied, in fact or in law, relative to any prize.

Remember, your entry must be postmarked no later than February 20, 1983.

ENTRY FORM
Contest 1 for the Best Drawings or Paintings

Attach this entry form, or a copy containing the same information, to *each entry* you submit. Read the instructions on page 90 and the Contest Rules on page 92 before you fill out this form.

Name _____

Address _____

City or Town _____

State _____ Zip _____

Telephone _____

Tell us something about your drawing or painting. We would like to know what the subject is, where it was drawn, why you chose to draw this particular subject. If you need more space, please use a separate sheet of paper.

_____

_____

_____

_____

_____

Attach this form with tape to the back of your entry. Protect your artwork with heavy cardboard when you wrap it for mailing. Please do not send frames or glass in the mail. Your entry should be addressed to:

Kids for Nature Contests
Sierra Club Books
530 Bush Street
San Francisco, CA 94108

ENTRY FORM
Contest 2 for the Best Photographs

Attach this entry form, or a copy containing the same information, to *each entry* you submit. Read the instructions on page 91 and the Contest Rules on page 92 before you fill out this form.

Name _____

Address _____

City or Town _____

State _____ Zip _____

Telephone _____

Tell us about your photograph: what is in it, where you took it, when you took it. If you need more space, please use a separate sheet of paper.

_____

_____

_____

_____

_____

Attach this form with tape to the back of your entry. Protect your photograph with heavy cardboard when you wrap it for mailing. Please do not send frames or glass in the mail. Your entry should be addressed to:

Kids for Nature Contests
Sierra Club Books
530 Bush Street
San Francisco, CA 94108

More Answers

The four sounds to see on page 45 are: ring, rower (roar), bark, creek (creak).

Elephant Pie, page 55

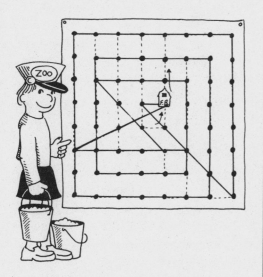

Zoo Puzzle, page 66

ENTRY FORM
Contest 3 for the Best Short Stories

Attach this entry form, or a copy containing the same information, to *each entry* you submit. Read the instructions on page 91 and the Contest Rules on page 92 before you fill out this form.

Name_____

Address _____

City or Town _____

State _____Zip _____

Telephone _____

Attach this form with tape to your entry. Your entry should be addressed to:

Kids for Nature Contests
Sierra Club Books
530 Bush Street
San Francisco, CA 94108

Remember, your entry must be postmarked no later than February 20, 1983.